E-journal Invasion

CHANDOS
INFORMATION PROFESSIONAL SERIES

Series Editor: Ruth Rikowski
(email: Rikowskigr@aol.com)

Chandos' new series of books are aimed at the busy information professional. They have been specially commissioned to provide the reader with an authoritative view of current thinking. They are designed to provide easy-to-read and (most importantly) practical coverage of topics that are of interest to librarians and other information professionals. If you would like a full listing of current and forthcoming titles, please visit our web site **www.chandospublishing.com** or contact Hannah Grace-Williams on email info@chandospublishing.com or telephone number +44 (0) 1865 884447.

New authors: we are always pleased to receive ideas for new titles; if you would like to write a book for Chandos, please contact Dr Glyn Jones on email gjones@chandospublishing.com or telephone number +44 (0) 1865 884447.

Bulk orders: some organisations buy a number of copies of our books. If you are interested in doing this, we would be pleased to discuss a discount. Please contact Hannah Grace-Williams on email info@chandospublishing.com or telephone number +44 (0) 1865 884447.

E-journal Invasion:
A cataloger's guide to
survival

HELEN HEINRICH

Chandos Publishing
Oxford · England

Chandos Publishing (Oxford) Limited
Chandos House
5 & 6 Steadys Lane
Stanton Harcourt
Oxford OX29 5RL
UK
Tel: +44 (0) 1865 884447 Fax: +44 (0) 1865 884448
Email: info@chandospublishing.com
www.chandospublishing.com

First published in Great Britain in 2007

ISBN:
978 1 84334 144 4 (paperback)
978 1 84334 193 2 (hardback)
1 84334 144 1 (paperback)
1 84334 193 X (hardback)

Typeset by Domex e-Data Pvt. Ltd.
Printed in the UK and USA.

To Igor and Anne.
Your support makes impossible look easy.
I love you.

Contents

List of figures and tables

Figures

Tables

About the author

Helen Heinrich's professional career spans two countries: the libraries of her native Russia and, today, the USA. She holds a bachelor's degree in library science from the St Petersburg State Academy of Culture (Russia) and a master's in library and information science from the University of California, Los Angeles. She is presently the cataloging coordinator at the California State University, Northridge; prior to this she was a serials cataloger at the Getty Research Library in Los Angeles. As a member of the Serials and Other Continuing Resources Standing Committee of the International Federation of Library Associations, she has been closely involved in shaping the committee's programs for the World Library and Information Congresses held at various cities around the world. Currently she serves as president of the Southern California Technical Processing Group, a regional affiliate of the American Library Association's Association for Library Collections and Technical Services.

The author may be contacted via e-mail at helen .heinrich@csun.edu.

Acknowledgements

My deepest gratitude goes to Stefan Klima, without whom my career in librarianship in the United States, as well as this book, would have been impossible. His mentorship, advice and encouragement have been my guiding light from the moment he took me on, newly arrived from Russia, as a volunteer at the Beverly Hills Public Library (BHPL) until the last question mark in this book. To my early concern that the BHPL readers would not understand my English, he replied with panache: 'Do not worry. I am from Britain and have been in this country for almost 20 years and still nobody understands me!' Everything became easier from that moment on. His dedication to editing and providing suggestions for this book has been invaluable.

I would like to thank Sue Curzon and Doris Helfer from California State University, Northridge Library (CSUN) for their support and encouragement while I was writing this book. Also from CSUN, Eric Willis, to whom I am especially grateful for his help and guidance with technical issues, patiently breaking them down to an understandable level. Many thanks go to Mary Woodley for her insightful comments and willingness to share experience.

I am grateful to Ani Matosian from the Getty Research Library for her support and help with this project.

I extend my special appreciation to Glyn Jones from Chandos Publishing for his encouragement and understanding.

Thank you to all my family and friends who did not see or hear much of me for the past year and who are still willing to talk to me.

List of acronyms

AACR	Anglo-American Cataloging Rules
A&I	Abstract and Indexing
AMeGA	Automatic Metadata Generation Applications project
AMS	Access and Management Suite
BEAT	LC Bibliographic Enrichment Advisory Team
CatER	Cataloging Electronic Resources/Electronic Resource Display in OPAC Task Force
CONSER	Cooperative Online Serials
COUNTER	Counting Online Usage of NeTworked Electronic Resources
CSUN	California State University, Northridge
DCMI	Dublin Core Metadata Initiative
DLO	document-like object
DOI	digital object indentifier
ERCIM	European Research Consortium for Informatics and Mathematics
ERM	electronic resource management
FAQ	frequently asked question
FRBR	Functional Requirements for Bibliographic Records
GMD	general material designation
GPO	Government Publications Office
IFLA	International Federation of Library Associations and Institutions

ILCSO	Illinois Library Computer Systems Organization
ILL	interlibrary loan
ILS	integrated library systems
ISBD	International Standard Bibliographic Description
ISSN	International Standard Serial Number
jake	jointly administered knowledge environment
JSC	Joint Steering Committee for Revision of AACR
JWP	joint working party
LC	Library of Congress
LCRI	Library of Congress Rule Interpretations
LCSH	Library of Congress Subject Heading
MARBI	Machine Readable Bibliographic Information Committee
MARC	machine-readable cataloguing
MeSH	Medical Subject Headings
METS	Metadata Encoding and Transmission Standard
MFHD	MARC Format for Holdings Data
MINERVA	Mapping the Internet: Electronic Resources Virtual Archive
MODS	Metadata Object Description Schema
NCSA	National Center for Supercomputing Applications
NISO	National Information Standards Organization
OA	open access
OAI	Open Archives Initiative
OAI-PMH	Open Archives Initiative Protocol for Metadata Harvesting
OCLC	Online Computer Library Center
ONIX	ONline Information Exchange

OPAC	Online Public Access Catalog
PAMS	publication access management service
PCC	Program for Cooperative Cataloging
PDC	program discipline code
PLoS	Public Library of Science
PURL	persistent URL
RDA	Resource Description and Access
RLIN	Research Libraries Information Network
SAR	Series Authority Record
SciELO	Scientific Electronic Library Online
SDSU	San Diego State University
SGML	standard generalized markup language
SOH	Serials Online Holdings
SPARC	Scholarly Publishing and Academic Resources Coalition
SPS	Serials Products and Subscriptions
SRN	Serials Release Notification
SRW	Search/Retrieve Web Service
SS	Serials Solutions
SUSHI	Standardized Usage Statistics Harvesting Initiative
TLC	The Library Corporation
TOC	table of contents
UM	University of Michigan
UNL	University of Nebraska at Lincoln
XML	extensible markup language

Preface

This book addresses the issues of a practical application of
the theory and concepts of serials cataloging. It is intended
for cataloging managers charged with defining policy and
procedures in providing access to electronic journals, as well
as cataloging practitioners. The book provides detailed
guidance to implementation processes for commercially
available journal MARC records and electronic serial access
management services. It may also be useful for vendors
providing online journal services to libraries.

The rapid changes in the publishing world, arising from
the emergence of the online environment, present a
challenge to inherent issues of bibliographic control. The
existing cataloging data – and content standards conceived
for physical materials – cannot be applied to the online
environment without losing elements crucial to the
description and discovery processes. In order to adapt to the
new environment the main cataloging tool, the MARC
format, underwent changes to account for electronic
publications and the networked environment.

Undermining MARC's monopoly on resource description,
new metadata schemata, designed specifically for a digital
environment, begin to enter the scene. The creation of library
and non-library data standards is mutually influential. The
adaption of MARC to the XML environment, in the form of
MARCXML, and MODS exemplify the need for data
exchange between the wider non-library world and the
library itself.

The impetus for the development of Dublin Core, on the other hand, has been the lack of a web description standard other than MARC. However, the library community, on a par with the standard's non-library applications, adopted Dublin Core. Spurred on by the commercial online environment, ONIX is finding its way into the library's electronic resource management toolbox. This book does not attempt to cover all metadata standards; rather it describes the ones that catalogers, especially serial catalogers, would most commonly encounter in their current work, as well as emerging developments in application of metadata schemata. It also presents what the author hopes is a balanced assessment of the standards that would be helpful in making a choice of metadata schema pertinent to a library's goals.

In giving an overview of the changes to the Anglo-American Cataloging Rules, *Library of Congress Rule Interpretations* and the *CONSER Cataloging Manual*, it was not intended to present an electronic serials cataloging manual. There are excellent resources available to serve that purpose. Instead, the intention is to show practical aspects of applying the established cataloging rules.

The effects of online publishing reverberate most strongly in the practices of cataloging electronic serials. Libraries have to grapple with providing access to ever-growing numbers of online journals that come directly from the publishers themselves or are part of large aggregations. The book examines the commercial services assisting in various forms of access to online journals, as well as in managing the continuously morphing aggregations. This book will be especially useful as a step-by-step guide to integrating MARC records provided by Serials Solutions.

Finally, in giving an overview of the electronic technologies and initiatives that facilitate access to the resources and examining developments towards bringing cataloging theory and practice closer together, the author tries to peek into the future and suggest avenues for taking the proactive steps that will help catalogers and libraries, in general, stay ahead of the curve in serving our users.

How the internet changed the lives of catalogers

When lay people think about libraries and librarians, their thoughts slow down almost to a standstill. After all, our only contribution to the world of thrills was an inspiration for the action figure 'Shushing Librarian'. And is it not our mission, anyway, to accumulate centuries' worth of wisdom, layer upon layer, and make it available in an atmosphere conducive for study? It has been like that for hundreds of years. We catalogers, of course, know that appearances are deceiving and behind the scenes it was never as quiet as on the library's front line. We were inventing new ways of organizing old knowledge, and had heated discussions about it.

Major jolts to the cataloging profession used to be rare and far apart. Perhaps the invention of paper in China over 1,900 years ago, Gutenberg's movable printing press in 1436 and then the card catalog as a retrieval device count among the few. Some countries, for example Russia, believed so much in the stability of the profession that even during the last decades of the twentieth century library schools there nurtured a special cataloging skill called 'library hand'. It was designed to teach catalogers to fill out library cards legibly for easy retrieval. The author knew better – and could never get beyond 'B' in learning that craft. And there we were, speedily writing those cards and competing with medieval monastery scribes in our imagination.

Then, almost overnight, the foundations were shaken and traditions were betrayed, and this does not mean typewriters or printed cards. The world of cataloging as we knew it ceased to exist with the emergence of machine-readable cataloging during the 1960s. The Library of Congress (LC) devised electronic formatting for bibliographic description, called MARC (machine-readable cataloging). As a descriptive standard the MARC format inherited from its predecessor, the library card, such functions as description and facilitation of resource discovery. The development of computer technology added the functions of resource identification in the context of shared cataloging and, related to that, the exchange of bibliographic data.

The structure of MARC followed the rules of the card catalog's description to reflect eight areas of the International Standard Bibliographic Description (ISBD): title and statement of responsibility; edition; material specification; publication and distribution; physical description; series; notes; standard number and terms of availability. The creation of MARC was a revolutionary development. It engendered the development of automated library systems, shared cataloging and bibliographic utilities such as the OCLC and RLIN. The impact of the invention of MARC was as transformative as the next shift of plates, which occurred with the advent of the internet in the 1990s.

Prior to the electronic format, the variety of cataloging materials was limited to the tangible media. There were MARC formats for printed books and periodicals, sound recordings, microfiche, etc. When the first digital editions began to appear, in the form of disks and then CD-ROMs, the MARC format and Anglo-American Cataloging Rules (AACR) were promptly amended to reflect the emergence of the new media.

No one, however, was prepared for what came with the emergence of the online environment – an avalanche of new types of publications that came mainly in the form of electronic journals. The tidal wave flowed in, drowning catalogers' efforts to stay above the water; not only did it never retreat, but it still continues its flow inland, making us paddle ever harder to safety, a haven known as full bibliographic control over online publications.

Why do we need to try so hard to provide catalog access to online publications when most of the holdings in libraries are still in print format and we lack resources to catalog fully even those? The answer lies in the nature of the library mission – to provide service and satisfy our users. And as numerous studies show,[1] the patron prefers virtual access to physical, thus making us spin the wheels chasing widespread desktop delivery. The challenge to provide access to the emerging online publications is one half of the problem. The other half occurred once publishers realized that online production was cheaper and the demand was increasing exponentially: they ceased to publish print versions and switched to online-only format. That was considered a major change, according to the Library of Congress Rule Interpretations (LCRI) 21.3B, and required a new record. Consequently, voluminous record maintenance, along with cataloging the new online material, became an integral part of the cataloger's workflow. As the number of online journals grew, so did the catalogers' workload, making it very difficult, and then impossible, to provide customary level catalog access to electronic serials.

MARC

At the dawn of the internet, MARC (www.loc.gov/marc/) was the only metadata[2] schema available to catalogers; its major role in bibliographic control is still uncontested and MARC remains the predominant format of library cataloging. The structure of the MARC record was developed in the late 1960s and followed ISBD description areas. It was designed for the data exchange technology of that era.

Organization of the record

The MARC record consists of the three parts: the leader, the directory and the variable fields.

The leader

The leader, as its name suggests, always comes first in the MARC record. Its length is fixed and takes the first 24 positions of the record. The leader contains information supplied by the computer and the cataloger. Its characters are either alphabetic or numeric codes and its main purpose is to provide data for machine processing.

Examples of computer-generated positions include 00-04 – Record length; 10 – Indicator count; 20 – Span of the length-of-field portion; 21 – Length of the starting-character-position portion, etc. Examples of cataloger-supplied data include 06 – Type of record; 07 – Bibliographic level; 17 – Encoding level; 18 – Descriptive cataloging form.

The directory

The directory follows the leader and is fully computer-generated. It lists tags, length and starting position for each variable field in the record.

The variable fields

There are two types of variable fields in the record: *variable control* fields and *variable data* fields. All tags are expressed by numbers, which makes MARC easily adaptable to library systems across the world without a need for translation.

Variable control fields are the 001–008 fields. They contain information necessary for machine record processing. Variable control fields are commonly referred to as *fixed fields*.

Variable data fields are the fields tagged 01x–8xx and comprise the bulk of the MARC record. Variable data fields contain data created by the cataloger:

01x–08x – Numbers, codes, classification

1xx – Main entry

2xx – Titles, editions, imprint

3xx – Physical description

4xx – Series

5xx – Notes

6xx – Subject headings

7xx – Added entries, linking fields

8xx – Series, location and holdings

9xx – Local fields.

Some of these fields are repeatable. Many variable fields have one or two single-digit indicators that allow more flexibility of information described and displayed in the corresponding field.

Updating MARC

The emergence of electronic resources, especially online publications, required an adjustment to the traditional MARC composition. New fields emerged, some old ones became obsolete and some codes were revised. In addition to numerous MARC variants for books, serials, maps and other formats, a category for electronic and, later, online resources was added.

Dating back to the 1960s, MARC format was not designed to provide bibliographic control for remote electronic resources. With the proliferation of online publications by the early 1990s, a pressing need emerged to amend the existing print-oriented MARC format and accommodate cataloging of online resources. As the uniform resource locator (URL) became the established tool for assigning internet addresses, it became imperative to allot a space in the record to indicate the location of the online resource. In 1993 the LC's Machine Readable Bibliographic Information (MARBI) Committee in its Proposal 93-4, 'Changes to the USMARC Bibliographic Format (Computer files) to Accommodate Online Information Resources',[3] introduced the new MARC field 856 to serve as a location for the resource's internet address. In addition, the proposal included adding four codes to 008/26 (Type of computer file) and changing the definition of two codes; broadening the use of field 256 (File characteristics) to include more specific descriptors and making field 516 (Type of file or data note) obsolete.

To test the usefulness and flexibility of MARC's amended coding and providing access to electronic resources, the Online Computer Library Center (OCLC), with funding from the US Department of Education Office of Library Programs, launched two successive projects spanning 1991 through 1996. The first, the Internet Resources Project, and the second, Building a Catalog of Internet Resources, also known as InterCat, had, among others, two very important objectives: 'to test the technical feasibility of providing automated access to electronic files based on coded access and location information provided in the bibliographic record (field 856)' and 'provide a Manual for Cataloging Internet Resources'.[4]

In the course of the InterCat project, librarians and information professionals worldwide were given the task of identifying, selecting and cataloging internet resources using MARC format and following AACR2 rules. The project resulted in the creation of an experimental database; by the time the project was completed the InterCat database contained over 45,000 records from more than 1,000 contributors.[5]

Another accomplishment of the project was the publication of *Cataloging Electronic Resources: OCLC-MARC Coding Guidelines*, by Rich Greene, in 1998. Later this manual served as a basis for the now widely used handbook *Cataloging Internet Resources: A Manual and Practical Guide* by Nancy B. Olson.[6]

A further change to MARC came in 1997 when the MARBI Committee revised the definition of code 'm' in leader 006 – Type of record,[7] allowing computer files to be coded for their most significant aspect. This means that if the intellectual content of a computer file is more significant than its carrier, it should be coded as a language material, 'a', and not as software, 'm'. To account for the carrier, however, field 007 – Physical description fixed field, for computer files was made mandatory in any record for an electronic resource.

Cataloging internet resources presented challenges for MARC because the format was based on stable-information materials. Publishers with well-known conventions that catalogers could rely on continued publication of print resources. Take standard monograph and periodical publications as an example. One could count on them having a cover, spine, title page, numbered pages of text, etc. Not so for internet publications – the computer specialists who carried out the act of publishing had no regard to libraries as their primary consumer. It took quite some time to adjust MARC to the online environment. The effort was aided by standardization of web publishing rules, traditional publishers going electronic and transferring print conventions to the online environment and the emergence of internet publications repeating the print format.

There are two principal resources for cataloging internet resources using MARC: Nancy B. Olson's aforementioned manual for non-serials and *CONSER Cataloging Manual*, Module 31, Remote Access Electronic Serials.[8] Both these publications are an amalgamation of the changes in cataloging standards that took place with the emergence of the internet. They build on Rich Greene's coding guidelines, guidelines issued by the OCLC and the LC Network Development and MARC Standards Office[9] and the adoption by IFLA (International Federation of Library Associations) of the ISBD (ER)[10] in 1997. They also reflect the 2001 changes to AACR2 Chapter 9, 'Electronic resources', and the 2002 revision of AACR2 that established a concept of integrating resources, as well as corresponding MARC21 changes stemming from that.

MARC for electronic materials

The content populating the MARC fields in the records for remote electronic resources is governed by AACR2 Chapter 9 and *CONSER Cataloging Manual* Module 31, Remote Access Electronic Serials. The catalogers should describe the resource using the MARC fields established for all materials, with the exception for the fields that are specific to remote formats.

Table 1.1 is a prototype of a record for a digitally created remote-access monograph in PDF format. This example demonstrates that the majority of fields applicable for print format are retained in the record; the fields that are specific

Table 1.1   Prototype record for a digitally created remote-access monograph in PDF format

MARC fields	MARC fields specific to electronic resource
008 Fixed field **Type: a** ELvl: I Srce: d Audn: Ctrl: Lang: eng **BLvl: m** **Form: s** Conf: 0 Biog: Mrec: Ctry: cau Cont: GPub: f LitF: 0 Indx: 0 Desc: a Ills: Fest: 0 DtSt: s Dates: 2005	**Type of record 'a'** – *'language material', i.e. intellectual content of the resource is more important than its carrier* **Bibliographic level 'm'** – *monograph* **Form of item 's'** – *electronic resource*
006 Computer file **[T006: m]** Audn: **File: d** GPub: 007 c $b r $d c $e n	006 – *Additional material characteristics, coding for electronic carrier* **Type of computer file 'd'** – *indicating that this is a document* 007 – *Physical description* **Category of material 'c'** – *computer file* **Specific material designation 'r'** – *remote-access resource* **Color 'c'** – *multicolored* **Dimensions 'n'** – *not applicable; always for remote-access resources*
040 LIB $ LIB	
043 n-us---	
090 Z695.24 $b L37 2005	
100 1 Last name, first name.	
245 10 Electronic monograph $h [electronic resource].	$h [electronic resource] – **GMD** (general material designation) 'electronic resource' in brackets in title statement
250 2nd ed.	
260 Los Angeles, Calif.: $b Publishing house, $c 2005.	
300 Optional	*Previously **300** not allowed for remote-access electronic resources; now optionally can be applied (AACR2 9.5B3)*

Table 1.1	Prototype record for a digitally created remote-access monograph in PDF format (*Cont'd*)
538 System requirements: Adobe Acrobat Reader.	*Special program needed for viewing this resource*
538 Mode of access: World Wide Web.	**Mode of access note** – *required*
500 Title from PDF title page (viewed on 9 Jan. 2006).	**Source of title note** – *required; combined with* **Date viewed note** – *required*
650 _0 Cataloging of electronic books.	
856 40 $u http://www.cataloging.edu/ electronicmonograph.pdf	**Electronic location and access (856)** Indicator 1 – '4' – access method is HTTP Indicator 2 – '0' – indicates that the address is for the resource itself

to remote-access monographs are highlighted and explained. Table 1.2 is a prototype of a record for a born-digital remote-access journal.

Undoubtedly, MARC is the predominant cataloging format in the library world. Librarians invented MARC for self-serving purposes and indisputably remain the only ones who can use it. In the words of Roy Tennant, user services architect at California Digital Library, 'There are only two kinds of people who believe themselves able to read a MARC record without referring to a stack of manuals: a handful of our top catalogers and those on serious drugs.'[11] However, even in the library, the main user of the format, there are many discussions regarding the merits of MARC. Features considered advantageous by some are viewed by others as having limitations. For example, is the often-mentioned complexity of the format beneficial or detrimental for its use? Is the high level of training required for MARC cataloging a

Table 1.2   Prototype of a record for a born-digital remote-access journal

MARC fields	MARC fields specific to electronic resource
008 Fixed field **Type: a** ELvl: Srce: d GPub: Ctrl: Lang: eng **BLvl: s Form: s** Conf: 0 Freq: m Mrec: Ctry: cau S/L: 0 **Orig: s** EntW: Regl: r ISSN: Alph: Desc: a **SrTp: p** Cont: 0 **DtSt: c Dates: 2000,9999**	**Type of record 'a'** – *language material* **Bibliographic level 's'** – *serial* **Form of item 's'** – *electronic* **Form of original item 's'** – *electronic* **Type of continuing resource 'p'** – *periodical*
006 Computer file **[T006: m]** Audn: **File: d** GPub: F	Additional material characteristics, *coding for electronic carrier* **Type of computer file 'd'** – *indicating that this is a document*
007 c $b r $d c $e n	007 Physical description **Category of material 'c'** – *computer file* **Specific material designation 'r'** – *remote-access resource* **Color 'c'** – *multicolored* **Dimensions 'n'** – *not applicable; always for remote-access resources*
022 1234-5678	Electronic ISSN
040 LIB $ LIB	
090 Z695.712	
245 00 Online journal $h **[electronic resource]**.	**$h [electronic resource] – GMD** *(general material designation) 'electronic resource' in brackets in title statement*
246 1 _$i Header title: $a Internet journal	*Title as found on the header*
260 Los Angeles, Calif.: $b Online publishing, $c 2000-	

Table 1.2   Prototype of a record for a born-digital remote-access journal (*Cont'd*)

[NO 300]	*CONSER 31.12 does not allow option given in AACR2 9.5B3*
310 Monthly	
362 0 _ Vol. 1, no. 1 (Jan. 2000) –	
500 Title from home page (viewed 11 Jan. 2005).	**Source of title note** – *required for all electronic resources; description based on note required for all remote-access resources when not cataloging from the first issue*
500 Latest issue consulted: Vol. 5, no. 1 (Jan. 2005).	**Latest Issue consulted note** – *used when more than one issue consulted*
538 Mode of access: World Wide Web.	**Mode of access note** – *required for all remote-access resources*
650_0 Cataloging of electronic journals $v Periodicals.	
856 40 $u http://www. onlinejournal.org $z Connect to online resource.	**Electronic location and access (856)** Indicator 1 – '4' – access method is HTTP Indicator 2 – '0' – indicates that the address is for the resource itself $z *Public note – optional*

problem or a blessing that ensures cooperation of only well-trained professionals? Is the rigidity of MARC a disadvantage or is it assurance of uniformity, which is the lifeline of the shared cataloging environment? But is MARC indeed so inflexible that it attracts so much criticism for this? Considering the age of the format and all the changes in technology that have taken place since its inception MARC is, in fact, remarkably flexible. It evolved, adapted and mutated as demanded, and it is still the strongest player in the field. How many other data standards have survived 40 years and still continue to prosper with no real competition? Is such stability considered a strength or a weakness? Does it mean that something was done very right a long time ago, or is it an indicator that catalogers are unwilling to change? Probably it is a little bit of both.

At the same time, during periods of rapid technological advances MARC often gets criticized for lagging behind the changes. In his article aptly entitled to describe his view that 'MARC must die', Roy Tennant outlines the features that stand in the way of progress.[12] Broaching the topic of extensibility of MARC, Tennant points out its flat, non-hierarchical nature and technical marginalization caused by library-only use of the standard. He called for the library community to be in step with the wider information technology industry and develop an XML-based encoding standard that will provide power and flexibility.

On the other side of the argument there are some eloquent voices in defense of the MARC21 format, asserting that it is misunderstood and underestimated. Martha Yee, for example, groups the problems attributed to the MARC21 format into four categories.[13]

- Problems that are not the fault of MARC21, but rather stem from data content standards, or cataloging rules of AACR2 and data value standards, such as 'name authority file' and LCSH (Library of Congress Subject Heading).

- Problems that are not problems at all, such as complexity, redundancy, lack of flexibility and extensibility. Yee points out that most of the complexity is optional and redundancy is justified since data recorded in different ways carry different functions. Too much flexibility and extensibility may result in a breakdown of the format standardization.

- Problems connected with the current shared cataloging environment, such as the high cost of authority control and so-called 'multiple version' problems linked to differentiation between two different expressions of the same work and two manifestations of the same expression.

- The MARC21 'shopping list', or other problems with MARC21 and vendor implementation. Here Yee identifies problems related to the language of headings, access to data in fixed fields and other problems connected with systems design. She also provides further recommendations for the improvement of the MARC tag set, such as adding separate fields for proper names as topical subject headings, cataloger-supplied expression information and separate subfields for the forename and surname.

In addressing the fear of bibliographic data marginalization, Yee makes a point that, unlike commercial information portals, library information is under authority control. This advantage makes searching library catalogs so precise. Perhaps the rest of the world is on its way to recognizing the importance of normalized data, similar to its discovery of metadata.

The format the chapter refers to, which is currently in use by the American library community, is called MARC21; born in 1998 from the merger of US MARC and CAN MARC, it has more than 2,000 fields and subfields, making it a highly pliable metadata set. It seems the format has a provision for every variation of the bibliographic entity. Having 2,000 fields at their disposal, the interesting question is how many of those do practitioners find useful and usable? Does an average well-trained cataloger need to know all 2,000 fields?

The University of North Texas, with a grant from the US Federal Institute of Museum and Library Services, is conducting a study on MARC content designation utilization (MCDU). The idea grew out of an earlier project undertaken by the university in 2003, the Z-Interop Project that analyzed 400,000 MARC bibliographic records from the OCLC's WorldCat database to establish the Z39.50 interoperability test-bed. The results showed that less than 50 per cent of nearly 2,000 MARC21 fields/subfields occurred even once in the records, and only 36 of the MARC fields/subfields accounted for approximately 80 per cent of all use.[14] To arrive at reliable results the MCDU project intends to analyze 56 million OCLC records, separating them between LC and other OCLC member libraries. It will be interesting to see if there is a gap between LC utilization of MARC and that of other libraries. One of the deliverables defined by the project team is the identification of 'core' elements in bibliographic records based on occurrence in the large sample of records and examination of initiatives recommending core bibliographic records.[15]

During MARC's 40-year history research has been limited, with no large-scale studies testing the proportion of fields used. Crawford and colleagues undertook one of the earliest studies,[16] and a second was carried out in Germany in 1997 by Bernhard Evensberg at the University of Braunschweig.[17] Evensberg analyzed over 4 million bibliographic records and identified the top 33 MARC fields used by catalogers. Only four fields occurred in 100 per cent of the records: 245, 260, 300, 050; and the last seven of the 'top' 33 fields, 653, 655, 630, 060, 810, 730, 533, occurred only in 1 per cent of the records. The MCDU project is the first to conduct the study in the internet-age environment that brought new challenges to MARC. The results of the empirical study notwithstanding, there is ongoing work on the part of the LC in the form of *access-level* records that codify what has been learned by practitioners. Provision of access to online and tangible resources can be expedited by using only a limited number of fields without significant detriment to the user's discovery process.

MARC21 is a complex schema developed for application to tangible materials. Inherently, the developments in internet technology made it difficult for the format to keep up with new functionalities of the web and data exchange between library and non-library sectors. The emerging online resources could not be fully expressed; furthermore, the resulting data could not be effectively exchanged via the MARC21 format. To improve communication between MARC and non-MARC resources and provide access to online materials through original description, the LC adopted XML (www.loc.gov/standards/marcxml/) as a framework for the networked environment.

MARCXML

XML (Extensible Markup Language) is born of a marriage of SGML (Standard Generalized Markup Language) and the web. HTML can't do much more than describe the look of a web page, whereas SGML is too complicated and unwieldy for most applications. XML achieves much of the power of SGML without the complexity and adds web capabilities beyond HTML.[18]

With the proliferation of XML as a mark-up language and its acceptance as a language of the internet, capable of encoding various digital objects, it seemed only natural that the library community would look to adapting some form of it for its own use.

In June 2002 the LC Network Development and MARC Standards Office announced the release of a schema for mapping MARC21 records into an XML environment for use in communicating these records. Since MARC21 can be fully expressed in XML, there is no data loss resulting from such conversions; in other words, MARCXML provides full 'roundtripability' of the conversion of MARC21 and XML schema without loss. Because of the XML flexibility there is no need to change the XML schema if changes occur in MARC standards. MARC data expressed in XML can be used where full MARC records are needed or can act as a 'bus' to enable MARC data records to go through further transformations, such as to Dublin Core and/or processes like validation (Figure 1.1).[19]

Adoption of XML schema for MARC21 not only allows transformation of MARC records into other metadata such as Dublin Core and MODS (Metadata Object Description Schema); it also allows conversion of XML-based records into MARC21 for use in integrated library systems (ILS). In fact, it is assumed that the conversion of MODS into MARC21 has to go through the step of converting MODS

Figure 1.1 MARCXML data act as a 'bus' for MARC21 records

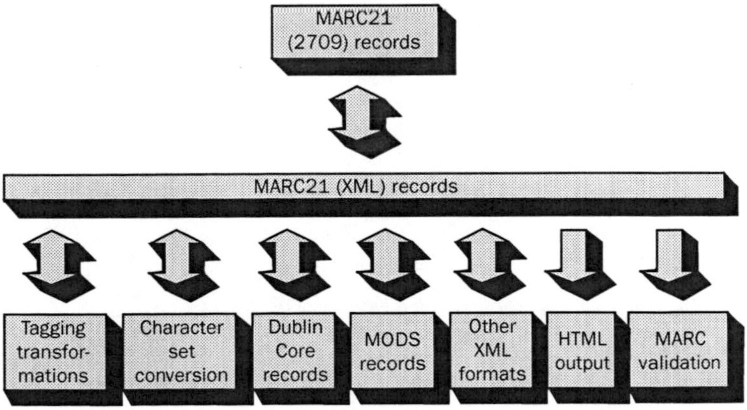

Source: Library of Congress MARCXML website

into MARCXML and only after that into MARC21. Thus the creation of MARCXML significantly advanced the interoperability of standards and promoted the use of vast quantities of data stored in MARC21 records in library catalogs (Figure 1.2).

Figure 1.2 Example of a MARCXML record

```
—<collection>
 – <record>
      <leader>01142cam 2200301 a 4500</leader>
      <controlfield tag="001">92005291</controlfield>
      <controlfield tag="003">DLC</controlfield>
      <controlfield tag="005">19930521155141.9</controlfield>
      <controlfield tag="008">920219s1993 caua j 000 0 eng</controlfield>
      -<datafield tag="010" ind1=" " ind2=" ">
      <subfield code="a">92005291</subfield>
    </datafield>
 –    <datafield tag="020" ind1=" " ind2=" ">
      <subfield code="a">0152038655:</subfield>
      <subfield code="c">$15.95</subfield>
      </datafield>
 – <datafield tag="040" ind1=" " ind2=" ">
      <subfield code="a">DLC</subfield>
      <subfield code="c">DLC</subfield>
      <subfield code="d">DLC</subfield>
    </datafield>
 – <datafield tag="042" ind1=" " ind2=" ">
 <subfield code="a">lcac</subfield>
 </datafield>
 – <datafield tag="050" ind1="0" ind2="0">
      <subfield code="a">PS3537.A618</subfield>
      <subfield code="b">A88 1993</subfield>
    </datafield>
 – <datafield tag="082" ind1="0" ind2="0">
 <subfield code="a">811/.52</subfield>
 <subfield code="2">20</subfield>
 </datafield>
 – <datafield tag="100" ind1="1" ind2=" ">
      <subfield code="a">Sandburg, Carl,</subfield>
      <subfield code="d">1878-1967.</subfield>
 </datafield>
 – <datafield tag="245" ind1="1" ind2="0">
   <subfield code="a">Arithmetic /</subfield>
 – <subfield code="c">
      Carl Sandburg; illustrated as an anamorphic adventure by Ted Rand.
      </subfield>
```

Figure 1.2   Example of a MARCXML record (*Cont'd*)

```
</datafield>
– <datafield tag="250" ind1=" " ind2=" ">
      <subfield code="a">1st ed.</subfield>
   </datafield>
– <datafield tag="260" ind1=" " ind2=" ">
      <subfield code="a">San Diego :</subfield>
      <subfield code="b">Harcourt Brace Jovanovich,</subfield>
      <subfield code="c">c1993.</subfield>
   </datafield>
– <datafield tag="300" ind1=" " ind2=" ">
      <subfield code="a">1 v. (unpaged) :</subfield>
      <subfield code="b">ill. (some col.) ;</subfield>
      <subfield code="c">26 cm.</subfield>
   </datafield>
– <datafield tag="500" ind1=" " ind2=" ">
<subfield code="a">One Mylar sheet included in pocket.</subfield>
</datafield>
– <datafield tag="520" ind1=" " ind2=" ">
– <subfield code="a">
A poem about numbers and their characteristics. Features anamorphic, or distorted,
drawings, which can be restored to normal by viewing from a particular angle or by
viewing the image's reflection in the provided Mylar cone.
   </subfield>
   </datafield>
– <datafield tag="650" ind1=" " ind2="0">
      <subfield code="a">Arithmetic</subfield>
      <subfield code="x">Juvenile poetry.</subfield>
   </datafield>
– <datafield tag="650" ind1=" " ind2="0">
      <subfield code="a">Children's poetry, American.</subfield>
   </datafield>
– <datafield tag="650" ind1=" " ind2="1">
      <subfield code="a">Arithmetic</subfield>
      <subfield code="x">Poetry.</subfield>
   </datafield>
– <datafield tag="650" ind1=" " ind2="1">
      <subfield code="a">American poetry.</subfield>
   </datafield>
– <datafield tag="650" ind1=" " ind2="1">
      <subfield code="a">Visual perception.</subfield>
   </datafield>
– <datafield tag="700" ind1="1" ind2=" ">
      <subfield code="a">Rand, Ted,</subfield>
      <subfield code="e">ill.</subfield>
   </datafield>
   </record>
</collection>
```

Source: Library of Congress MARCXML website

The LC provides a MARCXML toolkit to facilitate conversion of MARC21 to MARCXML (www.loc.gov/standards/marcxml/), as well as stylesheets for converting MARCXML to MODS, Dublin Core and other schemata.

MODS

MODS (www.loc.gov/standards/mods/) stands for Metadata Object Description Schema and represents a descriptive metadata standard. In the words of Rebecca Guenther, one of MODS designers, 'MODS is an XML schema that includes a subset of data elements derived from MARC21. It is intended to carry selected data from existing MARC21 records as well as to enable the creation of original resource description records.'[20] It was developed by the LC Network Development and MARC Standards Office in response to the need for an XML-based schema compatible with MARC21 but simpler in structure and with fewer elements than MARCXML. Due to its compatibility with MARC21, this schema is very conducive to use with library data. 'MODS... should provide an alternative between a very simple metadata format with a minimum of fields and no or little substructure (for example, Dublin Core) and a very detailed format with many data elements having various structural complexities such as MARC21.'[21] Because of its hierarchical structure MODS is particularly effective for coding complex objects for digital libraries, although it can also be used for non-digital materials. MODS maintains the semantics of MARC formatting while being more user-friendly because it has language-based, rather than numerical, tags. Language-based tags simplify utilization of the schema and shorten the training period. However, since the schema was created by English speakers, the language itself may present a challenge for foreign speakers and slow adoption of the standard abroad. One of the reasons for the international appeal of Dublin Core has been its translation into many foreign languages, while MODS so far is available in the English version only. The first version of MODS (MODS 2.0) became available for use in February 2003. The schema is now up to version 3.1, released in July 2005.

MODS is a subset of MARC and contains a selective number of MARC elements. Fewer MARC elements meant that some were combined and some dropped altogether.

The current version of MARC21 reflects the evolution of the standard since the 1970s. Elements carrying similar information but added to the MARC standard at different times are scattered throughout the record, causing redundancy and duplication. MODS, being a modern standard developed for the digital environment, compensates for some shortcomings of MARC by combining several MARC tags into a single element. For example, the MODS tag <originInfo> contains place of publication information from the MARC fields 008, 044 and 260 subfield 'a'; publisher information from MARC 260 subfield 'b'; date information from MARC 260 subfield 'c' and fields 033 and 008; edition information from MARC 250; and issuance/frequency information from the MARC leader and fields 310 and 321 (Figure 1.3).[22]

Because there are fewer elements in MODS than in MARC, round-trip conversion without loss is not possible between MARC21 and MODS. Records can be converted from MARC21 to MODS with no loss of data, but they cannot equally be converted from MODS to MARC21.

MODS contains 20 high-level elements and 47 sub-elements. Descriptive elements share definitions with equivalents in MARC. Another feature of MODS is the reuse of elements throughout the schema, where the same MODS

Figure 1.3	Contents of <originInfo> tag in MODS record containing information from several MARC fields

```
<originInfo>
_<place>
<placeTerm authority="marccountry" type="code">nyu</placeTerm>
</place>
_<place>
<placeTerm type="text">Ithaca, N.Y</placeTerm>
</place>
<publisher>Cornell University Press
</publisher>
<dateIssued>c1999</dateIssued>
<dateIssued encoding="marc">1999
</dateIssued>
<issuance>monographic</issuance>
</originInfo>
```

elements can be repeated as elements and sub-elements. As with MARC, MODS does not require usage of AACR2 or any other description standard; however, it can support AACR-based description as well as authority-controlled headings.

Figure 1.4 is an illustration of MODS top-level elements with selective examples of hierarchical sub-elements. Note that the element 'relatedItem' and its sub-elements are of particular interest: the sub-elements are the reused top-level elements of the schema, which allows for fully embedded description of another object within the main record.

Since MODS is MARC21 and XML metadata, it can be used as a crosswalk between MARC and non-MARC XML descriptions. Other potential uses of MODS include:

- a rich (but not too rich) XML metadata format for emerging initiatives, e.g.
  - SRW (Search/Retrieve Web Service), which uses Z39.50 and defines a search service that specifies metadata

Figure 1.4 Illustration of MODS top-level elements with selective examples of hierarchical sub-elements

1. titleInfo
    Sub-elements
    title
    subtitle
    partNumber
    partName
    nonSort
2. name
    Sub-elements
    namePart
    displayForm
    affiliation
    role
    role term
    description
3. typeOfResource
4. genre
5. originInfo
6. language
7. physicalDescription
8. abstract
9. tableOfContents
10. targetAudience
11. note
12. subject
    Sub-elements
        topic
        geographic
        temporal
        titleInfo
        name
        geographicCode
        genre
        hierarchicalGeographic
            continent
            country
            province
            region
            state

Figure 1.4 Illustration of MODS top-level elements with selective examples of hierarchical sub-elements (*Cont'd*)

```
            territory
            county
            city
            island
            area
        cartographics
          scale
          projection
          coordinates
        occupation
13. classification
14. relatedItem
        Sub-elements
          titleInfo
          name
          typeOfResource
          genre
          originInfo
          language
          physicalDescription
          abstract
          tableOfContents
          targetAudience
          note
          subject
          classification
          relatedItem
          identifier
          location
          accessCondition
          part
          extension
          recordInfo
15. identifier
16. location
17. accessConditions
18. part
19. extension
20. recordInfo
```

schemata for retrieval; since it uses XML, an XML metadata schema is needed, and one compatible with library data such as MODS would be desirable;[23]

- METS (Metadata Encoding and Transmission Standard), an initiative of the Digital Library Federation, provides a framework for encoding metadata using XML language;

- OAI (Open Archives Initiative), which harvests data from multiple systems for wider availability; currently OAI-PMH (Open Archives Initiative Protocol for Metadata Harvesting) primarily harvests records in Dublin Core but it can also harvest other metadata if they are in XML format.

■ original resource description in XML syntax that is simpler than full MARC.[24]

Figure 1.5 gives an example of a MODS record.

Figure 1.5 MODS record for electronic serial

```
mods version="3.0" xsi:schemaLocation="http://www.loc.gov/ mods/v3
http://www.loc.gov/standards/mods/v3/mods-3-0.xsd">
- <titleInfo>
   - <title>
      Emergence and Dissolvence in the Self-Organization of Complex
Systems
   </title>
   </titleInfo>
- <name type="personal">
   <namePart type="family">Testa</namePart>
   <namePart type="given">Bernard</namePart>
- <role>
   <roleTerm>author</roleTerm>
   </role>
</name>
- <name type="personal">
   <namePart type="family">Kier</namePart>
```

Figure 1.5   MODS record for electronic serial (*Cont'd*)

```
      <namePart type="given">Lamont B.</namePart>
  – <role>
      <roleTerm>author</roleTerm>
  </role>
  </name>
  <identifier
  type="uri">http://www.mdpi.org/entropy/papers/e2010001.pdf</identifier>
  – <relatedItem type="host">
  – <titleInfo>
      <title>Entropy</title>
    </titleInfo>
 –<originInfo>
      <issuance>continuing</issuance>
  </originInfo>
  – <part>
  – <detail type="volume">
      <number>2</number>
    </detail>
  – <detail type="issue">
      <caption>no.</caption>
      <number>1</number>
  </detail>
  – <extent unit="page">
    <start>17</start>
    <end>17</end>
      </extent>
  <date>2000</date>
  </part>
  </relatedItem>
  </mods>
```

Source: Library of Congress, MODS official website

Since the official release of the MODS schema in 2002, the LC has been experimenting with use of the standard. The Audio-Visual Prototyping Project[25] that began in 1999 explored issues of digital preservation for audio, video and film collections. The project is developing approaches for the digital reformatting of moving image and recorded sound collections as well as studying issues related to 'born-digital' audio-visual content. The project uses MODS as its descriptive metadata. Objects that already have descriptive cataloging records in one of the library's databases may reuse the data after conversion from MARC to MODS with minimal data loss. In some cases original resource description is provided and a MODS template is used.[25]

The MINERVA project (Mapping the Internet: Electronic Resources Virtual Archive)[27] aims at archiving open-access materials from the web. The websites are collected by themes (e.g. Election 2000, September 11th, Election 2002), and each theme receives a collection-level record in MARC21 to be added to the LC's online catalog. Because of its compatibility with MARC, MODS is used to create records at title level (Figure 1.6). The LC is collaborating with the Internet Archive (Alexa), the State University of New York and the University of Washington to expand the

Figure 1.6 Example of record from the collection 107 Congress Web Archive

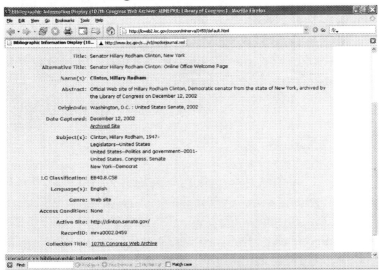

Source: Library of Congress MINERVA project

project. The latter two are assisting in identifying content and in using tools of their design to assign metadata descriptions to the websites collected.[28]

In the growing digital environment MODS has several advantages over MARC and other metadata schemata. It was designed specifically for online resources; it is XML-based which extends its use far beyond library catalogs; it is simpler than MARC but richer than Dublin Core; with language-based tags it is easier to use than MARC numeric values; the biggest advantage of all is its compatibility with MARC format, a cornerstone of a library's investment in cataloging. All this forecasts a big future for the standard.

> MODS is viewed as providing an evolutionary pathway forward for libraries. It attempts to take into account the rapid increase in electronic resources, the community's deep economic commitment to MARC data elements, the proliferation of formats and schemata beyond the control of the library community, and the rapidly growing XML tool environment. MODS derives from MARC21 while taking advantage of XML and the flexibility, tool development, and transformation options it offers.[29]

Dublin Core

The MARC record emerged as a substitute for the library catalog card and reflected the material holdings of a library. Dublin Core (http://dublincore.org/) was developed specifically to provide metadata for information in an electronic format, or document-like objects (DLOs). Yet, in internet years, Dublin Core is already an old standard.

The expansion of the internet during the 1990s resulted in improvement in the quality of online resources. As more authoritative data were published online, it became clear that search engines and indexing services could not be relied upon for the resource discovery process. In their turn, information providers felt an increased pressure to be found amidst the turmoil of the internet world. There arose a need for a standard in resource description, a metadata schema, simple and pliable enough to cope with a wide range of users.

The question arose: could MARC fit the bill? Was it possible to have an army of professional catalogers catalog the web? With all its value and indispensability for libraries – and precisely because of that – MARC could not carry out the challenge. MARC is costly, proprietary, labor-intensive and time-consuming. Its numeric tags, although not lacking worth, are not user-friendly and there is a requirement to adhere to description standards.

In the mid-1990s the cost of cataloging a record was $10; it continues to rise. At the same time there was no real need for a metadata schema that would fulfill all the functions of the MARC format. Specifically, there was no need to have a schema so detailed that it could aid the identification of a resource by comparing the physical object on hand with its description, an important shared-cataloging function of MARC. In the online environment a click of a mouse was enough to verify the match.

The main problem – and therefore the goal – of the resource description process was the discovery itself, with no need for identification and verification. Ideally, the schema ought to be simple enough to enable all authors to create metadata themselves, thus contributing to the prospective discovery of the resource at the time of its creation. To aid this process of author-created metadata, the element set had to be generic enough to act as a common denominator for all areas of knowledge. To round up a new metadata model wish-list, it also had to be open and compatible with various applications, and be potentially expandable to accommodate future growth in information needs.

The challenge was met by the OCLC and the National Center for Supercomputing Applications (NCSA). Together, in March 1995, in Dublin, Ohio, the two groups convened a workshop with 52 librarians, information professionals, scholars and programmers – 'geeks, freaks and people with sensible shoes', as they affectionately described themselves[30] – to design a simple set of metadata elements that would satisfy the needs of the various information communities.

After two days of consensus-building, the group emerged with a list of 13 core metadata elements. The term Dublin Core derives from the location of the meeting, Dublin, and Core, for the type of elements. The elements the group agreed on included *title, creator, subject, publisher, contributor, date, type, format, identifier, sources, language, relation* and *coverage.* Later this basic set expanded to 15 elements with the addition of two more tags – *description* (split from the subject element) and *rights.* The group decided that all elements would be optional, repeatable and can appear in any order. This was a big breakthrough and represented a major leap from the restrictions of the MARC format.

These 15 elements performed reasonably well, but they could not reflect the nuances of information. Increasing the number of elements would defeat the purpose of creating a simple set (and make the core part of the name a misnomer); it would make the schema unwieldy.

One of the original goals of the Dublin Core Metadata Initiative (DCMI), the body responsible for Dublin Core, was to create a schema with extensible elements so that it could grow without an increase to the main structure. Therefore, to meet the need for variations in the data being described, some elements were extended with qualifiers. To appreciate the flexibility of Dublin Core further, it is important to be aware of the 'dumb-down principle'. If during the resource discovery process an application encounters qualifiers that it cannot interpret (e.g. customized, newly established), it can use the main element as if it were unqualified, without significant loss of the core meaning.

Figure 1.7 shows the 15-element Dublin Core set, with qualifiers, all of which are subject to the 'dumb-down rule', as of July 2005.

The emergence of the new metadata schema for online resources resolved the need to create metadata, i.e. the cataloging process, in a way that was less costly and less intimidating. It eliminated the need for extensive training with its adherence to rigid cataloging rules and standards. In addition to creating only 15 optional and repeatable metatags, and the optional inclusion of existing description standards, the usage of controlled vocabularies was also left up to the metadata authors. Optional use of controlled vocabularies, such as Library of Congress Subject Heading (LCSH) or Medical Subject Headings (MeSH), made the Dublin Core schema a very attractive choice to various digitization projects. This flexibility eliminated the necessity for an expensive and highly complex segment of cataloging – the construction of pre-coordinated subject strings. It also allowed the use of lesser-known and 'home-grown' taxonomies, especially important for the projects of local historical societies, projects dealing with a very narrow subject or discipline and projects combining institutions with different missions, like libraries and museums. The idea behind the Dublin Core metadata was to create an easy-to-use set that could descibe major categories of an internet resource and help with the discovery process.

Figure 1.7 Dublin Core elements

Title

> Title.Alternative
> *Term description.* Any form of the title used as a substitute or alternative to the formal title of the resource. This qualifier can include title abbreviations as well as translations.

Creator

Subject

Description

> Description.TableOfContents
> *A list of subunits of the content of the resource.*
> Description.Abstract
> *A summary of the content of the resource.*

Publisher

Contributor

Date

> Date.Created
> *Date of creation of the resource.*
> Date.Valid
> *Date (often a range) of validity of a resource.*
> Date.Available
> *Date (often a range) that the resource will or did become available.*
> Date.Issued
> *Date of formal issuance (e.g. publication) of the resource.*
> Date.Modified
> *Date on which the resource was changed.*
> Date.dateAccepted
> *Date of acceptance of the resource (e.g. of thesis by university department, of article by journal, etc.).*
> Date.dateCopyrighted
> *Date of a statement of copyright.*
> Date.dateSubmitted
> *Date of submission of the resource (e.g. thesis, articles, etc.).*

Type

Format

> Format.Extent
> *The size or duration of the resource.*
> Format.Medium
> *The material or physical carrier of the resource.*

Identifier

> Identifier.BibliographicCitation

Figure 1.7 Dublin Core elements (*Cont'd*)

A bibliographic reference for the resource. Recommended practice is to include sufficient bibliographic detail to identify the resource as unambiguously as possible, whether or not the citation is in a standard form.

Source
Language
Relation

Relation.IsVersionOf
The described resource is a version, edition or adaptation of the referenced resource. Changes in version imply substantive changes in content rather than differences in format.
Relation.HasVersion
The described resource is a version, edition or adaptation of the referenced resource. Changes in version imply substantive changes in content rather than differences in format.
Relation.IsReplacedBy
The described resource is supplanted, displaced or superseded by the referenced resource.
Relation.Replaces
The described resource supplants, displaces or supersedes the referenced resource.
Relation.IsRequiredBy
The described resource is required by the referenced resource, either physically or logically.
Relation.Requires
The described resource requires the referenced resource to support its function, delivery or coherence of content.
Relation.IsPartOf
The described resource is a physical or logical part of the referenced resource.
Relation.HasPart
The described resource includes the referenced resource either physically or logically.
Relation.IsReferencedBy
The described resource is referenced, cited or otherwise pointed to by the referenced resource.
Relation.References
The described resource references, cites or otherwise points to the referenced resource.
Relation.IsFormatOf
The described resource is the same intellectual content of the referenced resource, but presented in another format.

Figure 1.7   Dublin Core elements (*Cont'd*)

> Relation.HasFormat
> *The described resource pre-existed the referenced resource, which is essentially the same intellectual content presented in another format.*
> Relation.ConformsTo
> *A reference to an established standard to which the resource conforms.*
> **Coverage**
> Coverage.Spatial
> *Spatial characteristics of the intellectual content of the resource.*
> Coverage.Temporal
> *Temporal characteristics of the intellectual content of the resource.*
> **Rights**
> Rights.AccessRights
> *Information about who can access the resource or an indication of its security status.*
> Rights.License
> *A legal document giving official permission to do something with the resource.*
> **Audience**
> Audience.Mediator
> *A class of entity that mediates access to the resource and for whom the resource is intended or useful.*
> Audience.EducationLevel
> *A general statement describing the education or training context.*
> **Provenance**
> **Rights holder**

Source: http://dublincore.org/documents/usageguide/qualifiers.shtml

Because of its simplicity and flexibility, the element set was embraced by the global information community. The DCMI became a truly international forum. In 2003 the International Standards Organization accepted the Dublin Core metadata set as a standard for resource description. Dublin Core has been translated into almost 30 languages, with more translations, including languages such as Burmese, Indonesian and Punjabi, under development.

On the organizational level, the DCMI counts among its participants Die Deutsche Bibliothek, the LC, the National Libraries of Australia, Canada and Finland, the OAI, the OCLC and many others.

Given its open-door policy and established international presence, Dublin Core functions as a common base for the myriad suppliers of electronic information. In the words of one of its creators, Diane Hillmann, Dublin Core is metadata pidgin for digital tourists.[31]

Figures 1.8 and 1.9 are examples of a Dublin Core record taken from the LC's Worthington Memory Digital

Figure 1.8   **Example of Dublin Core record, public view**

Source: Library of Congress website of Worthington Memory Digital Collection (www.loc.gov/catworkshop/readings/metadatabasics/examples/ worthingtonmemory.htm)

Figure 1.9 Example of Dublin Core record, metadata view

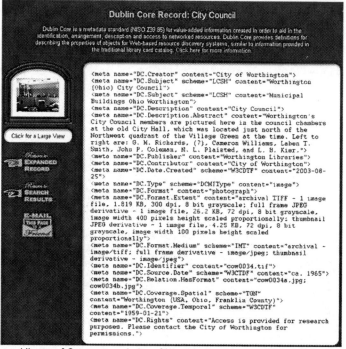

Source: Library of Congress website of Worthington Memory Digital Collection

Collection site. The first page presents the public display resulting from a underlying Dublin Core medatada; the second page shows the actual coding of information using the Dublin Core schema.

Another example of Dublin Core use in a digital library is a project of California State University, Northridge, which is chronicling the history of the San Fernando Valley, a suburb of Los Angeles. The San Fernando Valley History Digital Library (http://digital-library.csun.edu/SFV/) is a good showcase of how Dublin Core-based metadata can facilitate search and retrieval of online images. A populated set of labels describes the contents of an image and ensures that the information can be applied to each item consistently and, importantly, can be displayed next to the image.

The creation of the digital library was well described by Mary Woodley, the manager of the project, who documented 'best practices' regarding the name of the field, the order of display, whether or not the fields are under authority control, whether or not the fields are part of the metadata template and the definitions of how the fields are used.[32]

The number of fields per record in this collection ranged from Dublin Core's standard 15 to 24, and was determined by the need to record or display information required for identifying, retrieving or evaluating individual images, or by the need to record administrative or preservation information. For example, if related concepts needed to be labeled separately, one Dublin Core element could translate into several fields. Thus the labels were mapped to the Dublin Core elements, sometimes using one element to represent several labels. The project team took advantage of the fact that none of the Dublin Core fields was required but all were repeatable.[33] The terminology for display labels was based on Visual Resources Association standards, but included local definitions (Figures 1.10 and 1.11).

Straddling the worlds of traditional cataloging and non-library metadata, Dublin Core remains true to its original objective of being able to satisfy future information needs. At the DCMI meeting in Mexico in October 2006 the organization formed a new group to explore the emerging issues of social tagging (also called 'folksonomies', i.e. uncontrolled terminology assigned by users) and their application within the Dublin Core schema.

Despite successes, not everything envisioned by the creators of Dublin Core was realized. The idea for authors to create their own metadata in order to improve access to their work using the Dublin Core schema did not catch on

Figure 1.10 San Fernando Valley History project record, public view

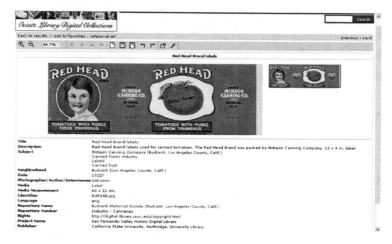

Figure 1.11 San Fernando Valley History project record, metadata view

California State University, Northridge

San Fernando Valley History Digital Library

Title:	Red Head Brand labels
Description:	Red Head Brand labels used for canned tomatoes. The Red Head Brand was packed by McKeon Canning Company. 13 x 4 in. label.
Subject:	McKeon Canning Company (Burbank, Los Angeles County, Calif.) Canned foods industry Labels Canned fruit
Neighborhood:	Burbank (Los Angeles County, Calif.)
Date:	1922?
Alternative Dates:	
Keywords:	
Photographer/Author:	Unknown
Donors & Others:	
Media:	Labels
Media Measurement:	60 x 11 cm.
Identifier:	BUR148.jpg
Language:	eng
Repository Name:	Burbank Historical Society (Burbank, Los Angeles County, Calif.)
Collection:	
Repository Number:	Industry - Canneries
Call Number:	
Finding Aid:	
Rights:	http://digital-library.csun.edu/Copyright.html
Project Name:	San Fernando Valley History Digital Library
Publisher:	California State University, Northridge, University Library.

fire as expected. The process was time-consuming and required at least some training. Furthermore, as pointed out by Jeffrey Beall,[34] the idea did not receive any encouragement from the designers of search engines like Google and Yahoo!

It quickly became clear that the creators, fluent in metadata authoring, could use their knowledge to manipulate search engines into placing their webpages at the top of the results display, a process that became known as spamming.

The idea of widespread author-created metadata has fizzled out for two reasons. On the discovery side the search engines, trying to reduce the incidence of tainted results, never supported it; on the creators' side the improvement in resource discovery by the same search engines made it unnecessary to structure the data in order for them to be found.

Reflecting on the decade of DCMI, Stuart Wiebel, former director of the initiative at the OCLC, said the expectations of Dublin Core users 'to have knowledge or patience to use it very well, seem touchingly naïve in retrospect'.[35]

Dublin Core remains a somewhat limited success with libraries as well. The element set is not detailed enough to capture the complexities of the description and there are no consistent instructions and documentation on the application of the tags. The fact that 'best practices' have to be developed by individual institutions deters its widespread use among libraries. In addition, the emergence of new standards, such as MODS, which are simpler than MARC but richer than Dublin Core, designed for digital environments and relate better to MARC may further undercut the proliferation of Dublin Core among libraries exploring digital projects.

ONIX

ONIX (ONline Information eXchange) is a standard developed by the publishing industry for providing product information to online book distributors. The goal was to provide as much information as possible to the online consumer in order to facilitate sales. ONIX is both a data dictionary of the elements which make up a product record and a standard means by which product data can be transmitted electronically.

ONIX (www.editeur.org/onix.html) was originally developed by the Association of American Publishers and EDItEUR, the international book and serials industry standards organization, and is now maintained by EDItEUR on behalf of the international publishing community. The ONIX standard is an XML schema utilizing language-based tags. ONIX version 1.0 was released in January 2000; the target audience was the publishing and book-trade industries. Gradually, the standard gained ground with the library community because of the long-standing relationships with publishers and book vendors.

The first efforts of the team who developed ONIX were aimed at devising description and transaction standards for books. However, soon after the release of the schema a parallel effort was launched to develop ONIX for Serials. This is a family of XML formats for communicating information about serial products and subscription information.[36] A joint working party (JWP) of members of the National Information Standards Organization (NISO) and EDItEUR was charged with the development of three application messages:[37] Serials Products and Subscriptions (SPS); Serials Online Holdings (SOH); and Serials Release Notification (SRN).

In a library context the SPS message relays information about serials titles subscribed to by the library, as well as subscription and pricing details. In the same manner the SOH format communicates information from a subscription vendor to a library about hosting services, publication access management services, agents or publishers. This format can be used to generate an alphabetical list of journal titles and for populating the knowledge base of a link resolver. The SRN provides information about the release of a serial issue. This notification can be used to update automatically the 'expected date' for print in the serials module of a library's ILS. Furthermore, electronic holdings can be updated by the link resolvers.

There is a broad potential for a library's use of the ONIX for Serials standard. Among the possible applications are communication of information about subscription packages available from a publisher or agent; information about journals contained in those packages; automated serials check-in; automated updates of online catalogs; and population and updating of link resolver knowledge bases.[38]

In recognition of the prospect of incorporating ONIX metadata into the work of libraries, the LC devised a stylesheet converting ONIX into MARCXML (www.loc.gov/standards/marcxml/). The LC has also taken the lead in applying ONIX to the repurposing of publisher records for its own catalog. The LC's Bibliographic Enrichment Advisory Team (BEAT) program, administered by the Cataloging Directorate (www.loc.gov/catdir/beat/), has been involved in an initiative to enrich MARC records by automatically adding tables of contents (TOCs) generated from the ONIX data. Approximately 50,000 ONIX TOCs have been created to date. Other LC projects using ONIX include:

- ONIX Reading Group Guides project – links catalog records to their associated reading group guides on the web;

- ONIX Descriptions project – creates records that contain a publisher's descriptions of its books;

- ONIX Sample Texts – makes links from LC catalog records to copies of sample texts from publishers (such as a first chapter, book jacket illustration, images, etc.);

- Contributor Biographical Information – ONIX data often include information about contributors, and BEAT has undertaken a biographical information initiative that makes this information available to researchers. The information is being linked from the catalog record to data stored on the web.

The adoption of a business standard such as ONIX into library use is, in the author's view, only one of the early examples of blurring lines between commercial enterprises and the library world. It represents the recognition of the fact that the organization of bibliographic information no longer lies solely within the library domain. Moreover, driven by the bottom line and having superior financial resources, as well as a nimble decision-making structure, the business community has the ability to take a lead in developing information standards that would benefit library applications. The increase in collaboration between the library and the business world will inevitably benefit the clients of both sectors.

Notes

1   Bane, A.F. (1995) 'Business periodicals Ondisc: how full-text availability affects the library', *Computers in Libraries*, 15(5): 54–6; Grefsheim, S., Franklin, J. and Cunningham, D. (1991) 'Biotechnology awareness study, part 1: where scientists get their information', *Bulletin of the Medical Library Association*, 79(1): 36–44; Hurd, J.M. and Weller, A.C. (1997) 'From print

to electronic: the adoption of information technology by academic chemists', *Science & Technology Libraries*, 16(3/4): 147–70; Curtis, K.L., Weller, A.C. and Hurd, J.M. (1997) 'Information-seeking behavior of health sciences faculty: the impact of new information technologies', *Bulletin of the Medical Library Association*, 85(4): 402–10; Pelzer, N.L., Wiese, W.H. and Leysen, J.M. (1998) 'Library use and information-seeking behavior of veterinary medical students revisited in the electronic environment', *Bulletin of the Medical Library Association*, 86(3): 346–55; Tomney, Hilary and Burton, Paul F. (1998) 'Electronic journals: a study of usage and attitudes among academics', *Journal of Information Science*, 24(12): 419–29.

2   Metadata – literally, 'data about data' – include data associated with either an information system or an information object for purposes of description, administration, legal requirements, technical functionality, use and usage and preservation. Baca, Murtha (ed.) (1998) *Introduction to Metadata: Pathways to Digital Information*, available at: *www.getty.edu/ research/ conducting_research/standards/intrometadata/index. html* (accessed: 12 November 2006).

3   Available at: *www.itcompany.com/inforetriever/marc934d. txt* (accessed: 12 November 2006).

4   Available at: *http://digitalarchive.oclc.org/da/ViewObject. jsp?fileid=0000003519:000000091690&reqid=5073* (accessed: 12 November 2006).

5   Available at: *www.oclc.org/research/publications/archive/ releases/1998-09-28.htm* (accessed: 12 November 2006).

6   Greene, Rich (1998) *Cataloging Electronic Resources: OCLC-MARC Coding Guidelines*. Dublin, OH: OCLC; Olson, Nancy B. (ed.) (1997) *Cataloging Internet Resources: A Manual and Practical Guide, 2nd edn.*

Dublin, OH: OCLC; available at: *www.purl.org/oclc/cataloguing-internet* (accessed: 5 December 2005).

7   Available at: *www.loc.gov/marc/marbi/1997/97-03.html* (accessed: 12 November 2006).

8   Olson, note 6 above; *CONSER Cataloging Manual, Module 31, Remote Access Electronic Serials.* Washington, DC: Serial Record Division, Library of Congress, updated 2004; available at: *www.loc.gov/acq/conser/Module31.pdf* (accessed: 18 February 2007).

9   Greene, note 6 above; Weitz, Jay (1998) *OCLC Guidelines on the Choice of Type and BLvl for Electronic Resources.* Dublin, OH: OCLC; Library of Congress Network Development and MARC Standards Office (1999) *Guidelines for Coding Electronic Resources in Leader/06.* Washington, DC: Cataloging Distribution Service, Library of Congress.

10 Available at: *www.ifla.org/VII/s13/pubs/isbd.htm* (accessed: 12 March 2007).

11 Tennant, Roy (2002) 'MARC must die', *Library Journal*, 127(17): 26, 28.

12 Ibid.

13 Yee, Martha M. (2004) 'New perspectives on the shared cataloging environment and a MARC21 shopping list', *Library Resources & Technical Services*, 48(3): 165–78; post print available free at: *http://repositories.cdlib.org/postprints/365*.

14 Available at: *www.mcdu.unt.edu/?p=9* (accessed: 21 January 2006).

15 Ibid.

16 Crawford Walt, Stovel, Lennie and Bales, Kathleen (1986) *Bibliographic Displays in the Online Catalog.* White Plains, NY: Knowledge Industry Publications.

17 Available at: *www.allegro-c.de/formate/formneu.htm#top33* (accessed: 12 March 2007).

18 Tennant, Roy (2001) 'Digital libraries – XML: the digital library hammer', *Library Journal*, 126(5): 30–2.

19 Available at: *www.loc.gov/standards/marcxml/marcxml-architecture.html* (accessed: 12 March 2007).

20 Guenther, Rebecca S. (2003) 'MODS: the Metadata Object Description Schema', *Portal*, 3(1): 137–50.

21 Ibid.

22 McCallum, Sally H. (2004) 'An introduction to the Metadata Object Description Schema (MODS)', *Library Hi Tech*, 22(1): 82–8.

23 Guenther, note 20 above.

24 Available at: *www.loc.gov/standards/mods/presentations/ala2005-mods_files/frame.htm* (accessed: 12 March 2007).

25 Available at: *www.loc.gov/rr/mopic/avprot/avprhome.html* (accessed: 12 March 2007).

26 Guenther, note 20 above.

27 Library of Congress (2006) 'MINERVA: Mapping the Internet Electronic Resources Virtual Archive'; available at: *http://lcweb.loc.gov/minerva/minerva.html* (accessed: 29 October 2006).

28 Guenther, note 20 above.

29 McCallum, note 22 above.

30 Wiebel, Stuart L. (2005) 'Border crossings: reflections on a decade of metadata consensus building', *D-Lib Magazine*, 11(7/8): 1–9.

31 Available at: *http://dublincore.org/documents/usageguide/* (accessed: 12 March 2007).

32 Woodley, Mary S. (2002) 'A digital library project on a shoestring', *Library Collections, Acquisitions, and Technical Services*, 26(3): 199–206.

33 Ibid.

34 Beall, Jeffrey (2004) 'Dublin Core: an obituary', *Library Hi Tech News*, 21(8): 40–1.

35 Wiebel, note 30 above.

36 Klemperer, Kathy (2006) 'Serials Standards Update Forum ONIX for Serials', paper presented at Annual Conference of American Library Association, New Orleans, 22–28 June.

37 Needleman, Mark H. (2005) 'ONIX for Serials – the NISO/EDItEUR joint working party', *Serials Review*, 31(4): 324–5.

38 Ibid.

2

New rules and issues for e-journals in the library setting

With the proliferation of different types of electronic resources, library and otherwise, and the development of innovative non-library metadata schemata, it was becoming clear that the principles for the content description of olden years could not keep up with new realities. The time came to refocus and adjust terminology, scope and approach to synchronize cataloging rules in line with the era of electronic resources.

Therefore, with this new perspective, in December 2002 the LC implemented revisions to the AACR.[1] The changes were the result of several years' work by the Joint Steering Committee for Revision of AACR (JSC), and affected some fundamental approaches to the description as well as terminology. Most rules did not change; however, Chapters 1, 3, 9, 12 and 21 underwent key modifications. In relation to electronic resources the changes to Chapters 9 and 12 were of paramount importance.

The founding principles of AACR2 were to describe a bibliographic item in hand. All items were tangible and stable, as were the cataloging rules themselves. The inconvenience of loose-leaf publications – the aberration of what a good publication should be – was dealt with in a monograph section, not because they belonged there but because there was no other place to tuck them in. Who knew that ever-changing loose-leaves were precursors of websites – unstable but always current? A loose-leaf publication to a webpage is what an abacus is to a calculator – same purpose but a different technology.

The most prominent change in the approach to item description was reflected in the revision of Rule 0.24. The new rule allowed using all aspects of an item as a basis of description, 'including its content, its carrier, its type of publication, its bibliographic relationships, and whether it is published or unpublished',[2] not the physical form of the item alone, as was the case before. As for modification of terminology, a major change took place throughout AACR2: the term 'computer file' was replaced by 'electronic resource'. This change was reflected in Chapter 1, Rule 1.1C1, in the form of the new general material designation (GMD) 'electronic resource'. Rule 9.5B1, physical description area, allowed the option of common usage terms, such as CD-ROM, DVD-ROM, for directly accessed electronic resources (and yes, not until 2002 were users allowed to understand what is hiding behind the arcane phrase 'computer optical disc').

AACR2: Chapter 9

The major revisions of Chapter 9 included a change of the chapter's name, from 'Computer files' to 'Electronic resources', and expansion of the scope of electronic resources to include data, programs or combinations of data and programs[3] that can be accessed either directly with a physical carrier like a CD-ROM or remotely through a connection to the network system.

The sources of information ('chief sources of information', Rule 9.0B1) was broadened to consist of the entire resource – not only title page, as it was before, but also main menus, homepage, the file header(s), encoded metadata, etc. and physical carrier of the resource. The only criteria for preferred source became the fullness of information. The edition statement (Rule 9.2B5) rule for the multiple physical carriers of the resource, for instance a set of CD-ROMs, now gives instructions to record the edition statement applicable to the entire resource, when the editions are given for the whole as well as parts of the resource. This part/edition-neutral approach cuts down the number of records and collocates a single resource on to one record; it is similar to the aggregator-neutral serial record adopted by CONSER, and signifies a practical take on cataloging.

According to the 2002 LCRI, area 9.3B1, describing the type and extent of the resource (formerly file characteristic area), was not to be used for electronic resources. Later, in 2004, amendments to the revision designated the entire 9.3 area – material (or type of publication) specific details – as not applicable to electronic resources. Another important change took place with Rule 9.4B2 (publication and distribution), which stated that all remote-access electronic resources are considered as published. A new rule, with the code 9.4F4, prescribed using the latest copyright date of any part of the resource if there was no publication/distribution date that applied to the resource as a whole.

A number of modifications were made to the note area (Rule 9.7). The 'mode of access' note was mandated to use the exact wording; some new examples were added to the title notes; and a new note (9.7B22), 'item described', was added to the rules. This rule mandated that the date when the resource was viewed was to be stated in the record.

Overall, the revisions to Chapter 9 were relatively minor, attending to the details that needed to be brought into synchronization with a world where computer files metamorphosed into electronic resources. The real changes, however, took place in Chapter 12.

AACR2: Chapter 12

The revisions to Chapter 12 arose from a paper on 'Issues related to seriality'[4] by Jean Hirons, at that time the LC CONSER coordinator, and Crystal Graham. The paper was presented at the 1997 Toronto Conference on the Principles and Future Development of AACR; in it, Hirons and Graham spoke of the need for AACR2 to address the issues of seriality. As a result the JSC requested Hirons to prepare a report with proposals covering both serials and integrating resources.[5] The results, emanating from discussions of the report, prescribed revisions of cataloging rules and were subsequently incorporated into the AACR2 2002 revision. Another impetus for revising Chapter 12 was the concurrent effort to harmonize AACR2 with the International Standard Bibliographic Description (for Serials) and the ISSN manual, particularly in the area of transcription series titles.

Chapter 12, formerly known to catalogers as the chapter on serials, underwent a major conceptual overhaul. The introduction of the new term 'continuing resources' as the name for the chapter as well as the concept itself signified a shift away from the prior division of information resources into 'monographs' and 'serials'.

Serials were not just renamed 'continuing resources'. Some materials, previously cataloged as monographs, found themselves included in this new expanded category. It is precisely the realignment of those materials, which were undergoing updates but were still considered monographic, that was the cause of a major change. Under the old rules materials such as updated websites and databases were cataloged as monographs because the major division of the resources was along the lines of whether ongoing changes and updates were issued in discrete parts or not (Figure 2.1).

Figure 2.1   Pre-2002 division of bibliographic materials

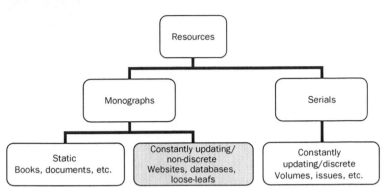

The new revision not only changed the approach to the division of bibliographic resources, it changed the definition of a bibliographic resource itself, bringing it closer to the terminology of Functional Requirements for Bibliographic Records (FRBR),[6] a framework developed by IFLA. According to the new definition, a bibliographic resource is 'an *expression* or *manifestation* of a work or an item that forms the basis for bibliographic description. A bibliographic resource may be tangible or intangible.'[7] The terms *expression* and *manifestation* parallel the terms of FRBR: work, *expression, manifestation* and item.

The new boundaries now lay within the intended extent of publication, its type of issuance – one time or ongoing. Ongoing publications were renamed 'continuing resources' and defined as 'a bibliographic resource that is issued over time with no predetermined conclusion'.[8] One-time publications with expected conclusions were named 'finite', with no definition in the AACR2 glossary.

Updated non-discrete materials, such as loose-leaf publications and websites, were divorced from monographs and became a new species – 'integrating resources'. They were defined as: 'integrating resource – a bibliographic resource that is added to or changed by means of updates that do not remain discrete and are integrated into the whole'.[9] To make matters more confusing, integrating resources can also be finite or continuing.

Continuing resources include serials and ongoing integrating resources. The new family tree of bibliographic resources now looks as shown in Figure 2.2.

Serials, formerly a resource type on its own, became part of continuing resources, and to reflect this acquired a revised definition: 'Serial – a *continuing resource* issued in a succession of *discrete* parts, *usually bearing numbering, that has no predetermined conclusion*. Examples of serials include journals, magazines, electronic journals, continuing directories, annual reports, newspapers, and monographic series.'[10] The words in italics emphasize the changes: *continuing resource* – a new class (previously *a publication*); *discrete* parts – to distinguish between non-discrete or integrating parts, such as websites (previously *issued in successive parts*); *usually bearing numbering* – previously *bearing numeric or chronological designations*; *that has no predetermined conclusion* – previously *intended to be continued indefinitely*.

Figure 2.2 Post-2002 division of bibliographic materials

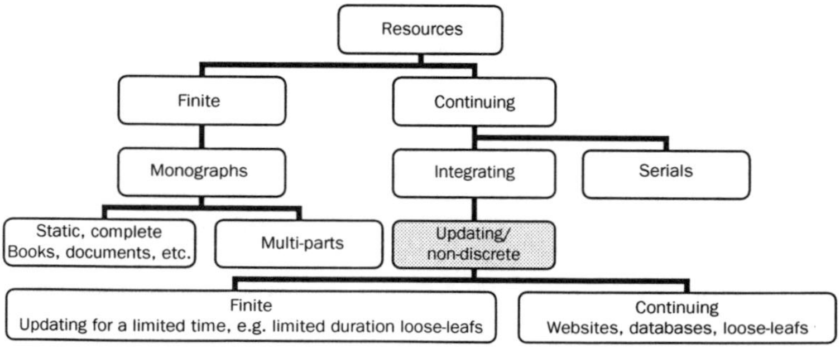

Chapter 12 covers continuing resources, i.e. all integrating resources, whether finite or continuing, and serials. It does not cover multi-part items because they are finite publications *and* their updates/changes remain discrete, which prevents them from being finite integrating resources.

It is not surprising that the new division has been confusing to catalogers. To clarify some of the confusion the LC expanded the scope of LCRI Rule 12.0A and replaced it by Rule 1.0 to provide guidance on the type of resource being cataloged. The main determination to be made before beginning cataloging, based on the type of issuance, is whether the resource is a monograph or a serial or an integrating resource. Tables 2.1–2.3 summarize the major characteristics that can help distinguish one type of material from another.

For print-format resources the new material classification made little difference, except moving the only printed integrating resource, loose-leaf, from monographs to integrating resources. The dividing lines between print resources remained clear, as before. The bigger challenge

Table 2.1   Serial versus integrating resource

Characteristic	Serial	Integrating resource
Type of update	Succession of discrete parts	Updates do not remain discrete and are integrated into the whole
Numbering	Usually bears numbering	No numbering
Duration	*Continuing* with no predetermined conclusion	May be *finite* with predetermined conclusion, or *continuing* with no predetermined conclusion
Edition	Numeric statement	Edition statement

Table 2.2 Monograph versus serial

Characteristic	Monograph	Serial
Frequency	Three or more years apart	Stated frequency; published no more than 1–2 years apart
Numbering	N/a	Numeric, alphabetic and/or chronological designation
Type of issuance	Complete, *finite*	No predetermined conclusion, *continuing*
Acquisition	Cannot be subscribed to	Subscription
Limited duration	No serials characteristics	Successive issues, numbering, frequency (e.g. bulletin of a non-recurring meeting)
Conference publications	Not ongoing Title unique to each issue Part of a numbered monographic series	Ongoing meeting

Table 2.3 Monograph versus integrating resource

Characteristic	Monograph	Integrating resource
Type of issuance	Complete, not changing	Updating by non-discrete parts
Finite resource	Complete in finite number of parts	Updating for a limited time

became determining the type of issuance for online resources. The lines are much finer there because online resources are fluid by nature and by definition defy the word 'complete'. Table 2.4 shows the guidance LCRI 1.0 offers for electronic resources.

Figures 2.3–2.7 show some examples illustrating online resources' types of issuance and explaining the rationale for determination.

Table 2.4 Summary of distinguishing characteristics of electronic resources

	Remote	Direct
Serial	Material added as discrete, usually numbered issues (an 'issue' can consist of a single article)	Resource carrier issued successively
Integrating resource	Material added, changed or deleted via updates that do not remain discrete	No direct access – resource is an integrating resource
Monograph	Resource complete in one part or intended to be complete in a finite number of parts, including those resources that are corrected via 'errata' information	

Figure 2.3 Electronic resources, identification of type

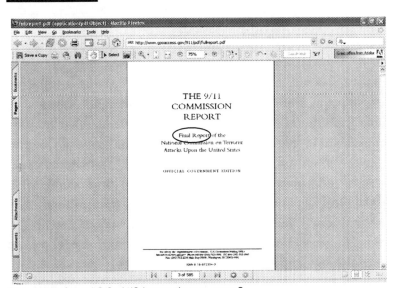

Step 1: Monograph? Serial? Integrating resource?
Step 2: Updating? No.
Step 3: If not updating, then finite resource, i.e. monograph.

Figure 2.4   Electronic resources, identification of type

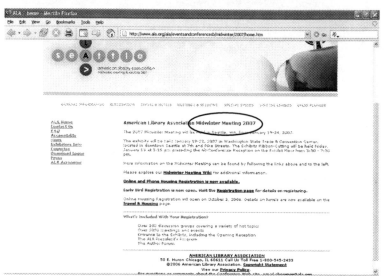

Step 1: Monograph? Serial? Integrating resource?
Step 2: Updating? Yes.
Step 3: If updating, it is a continuing resource.
Step 4: Do changing parts remain discrete? No.
Step 5: If changes do not remain discrete, it is an integrating resource.
Step 6: What kind of integrating resource: finite or continuing?
Step 7: It continues updating only for the duration of the conference.
Step 8: It has a predetermined conclusion, so it is a finite integrating resource.

In addition to serials and finite and continuing integrating resources, Chapter 12 also covers some publications of limited-duration activities. LCRI 1.0 explains what may be considered in this category. To be within the scope of Chapter 12, finite resources need to have some characteristics of serials, i.e. successive issues, frequency and numbering. Examples of limited-duration-activities publications may include daily bulletins of a non-recurring conference, a monthly report of a project or an annual report of an expedition. Chapter 12 does not include publications of five-year plans and census data, and does not permit the recataloging of old records. It also gives instructions to

| Figure 2.5 | Electronic resources, identification of type |

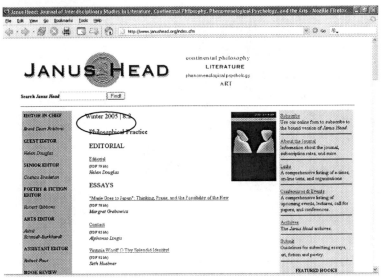

Step 1: Monograph? Serial? Integrating resource?
Step 2: Updating? Yes.
Step 3: If updating, it is a continuing resource.
Step 4: Do changing parts remain discrete? Yes, it has numeric designation of issues.
Step 5: If changing parts remain discrete and bear numeric designation, it is a serial.

catalog electronic resources that were published in print based on the type of issuance of the electronic resource, not the type of issuance of the print resource.

In addition to introducing the new concepts of continuing and integrating resources, another big change in the revision of AACR2 in 2002 was the concept of 'major versus minor change'. This revision was aimed at simplifying the code, taking into consideration a publisher's intention and reducing the number of new records and new ISSNs due to a change in title.

The newly introduced structure of the types of publications not only required a new cataloging approach and new rules to support it, but also prompted a series of changes to the existing rules. The revisions to Chapter 12

| Figure 2.6 | Electronic resources, identification of type |

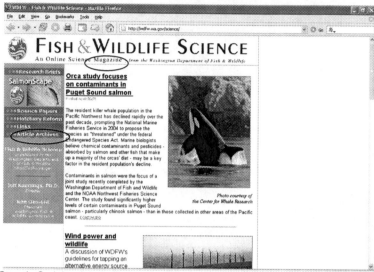

Step 1: Serial or integrating resource?

Step 2: Not sure, the subtitle has the word 'magazine', *but*...

Step 3: Changing parts do not remain discrete; there is no numbering. Articles are integrated into the whole as they become available (next image).

Step 4: Since articles are integrated into the whole and regardless of the word *magazine* in subtitle, it is an integrating resource.

brought changes to the existing rules for cataloging serials as well as the introduction of new rules for cataloging integrating resources. The revisions also absorbed some of the rules that were previously expressed through the LCRI.

Key changes to the previous rules are detailed below.

Area 1: Title and statement of responsibility

There was a change to the transcription of the title proper reflected in Chapters 1 and 12.

■ Rule 1.1B1, applicable to all types of materials, instructs omission of introductory words not intended to be part of the title, e.g. *Welcome to*...

Figure 2.7 Example of an integrating resource, called 'magazine'

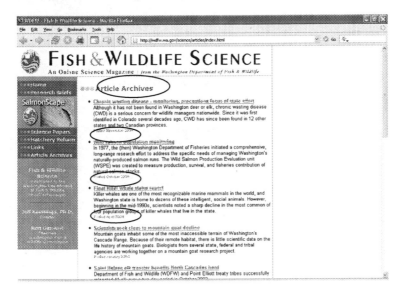

- Rule 12.B1 now reads that an obvious typographical error should be corrected and the correct form recorded in 245, while the found form with the mistake should be transcribed in 246.

- Rule 12.B2 states that if abbreviated and full forms of the title are available on the chief source, use the full form. This rule was the result of harmonization of AACR2 with such standards as ISSN and ISBD (CR).

Area 2: Numbering (applicable to serials only)

- Rules 12.3B1 and 12.3C1 stipulate that you should record numeric and/or alphabetic and chronological designation of a serial with the same terms but not necessarily with the same punctuation, for example a hyphen can now be changed to a slash.

- Rule 12.3C4 (previously in the LCRI only) codifies that if numbering repeats each year, the year should be transcribed before the number.

- Rule 12.3G1 conveys that there is no need to create a new record if the new numbering begins and there are no words like 'new series' present on the source.

- Rule 12.4F refers to 1.4F8 for recording the beginning date of publication as date of the issues published, not when the issue is designated as 'first'. If the description is not based on the first issue, probable beginning date can be supplied.

Area 4: Publication

- Rule 1.4D4 no longer allows shortening the publisher's name in 260 (so it can be searched).

- 1.4F8 in synchronization with CONSER practice instructs not to give the date in 260 if first or last issue is not in hand. The rule also disallows an ending comma in $b if no $c present, and incomplete brackets in $c. There is no requirement for ending punctuation.

Area 5: Physical description

- Rule 9.5B1 established the use of conventional terminology, e.g. CD-ROM and not 'computer optical disc'.

Area 7: Notes

- Rule 12.7B8 means there will be no reciprocal linking notes between monographs. However, linking relationships between other types of materials are allowed:
  - serials and serials
  - serials and integrating resources

- serials and monographs
- integrating resources and integrating resources
- integrating resources and monographs.

■ Rule 12.7B23 directs the cataloger to make a 'latest issue consulted' note if more than one issue has been consulted. As opposed to 'description based on' and source of title notes, the 'latest issue consulted' could not be combined and should always be recorded separately.

Other changes

The new Chapter 12, 'Continuing resources', encompasses both serials and integrating resources. While some rules for serials have been revised from the existing ones, a completely new set of rules had to emerge to cover new types of materials – integrating resources – and specify the difference in their treatment from that of serials.

Rule 12.0B1, 'Basis of description', introduces different rules for the two types of materials. Catalogers are instructed to continue using first or earliest available issue of serials as the basis for description. For integrating resources, conversely, the basis of description is the latest, *current iteration* of that resource.[11]

'Iteration' is another new concept in AACR2, and is defined as 'an instance of an integrating resource, either as first published or after it has been updated'.[12] In the words of Barbara Tillett, 'it's the snapshot in time that you see when you're looking at an integrating resource'.[13]

In contrast to serials and their successive-entry approach, when a new record is created every time a main entry changes, the description of integrated resources mandates an 'integrated entry', which is close to the latest-entry policy. Each integrated resource receives only one record, and when the description elements change the record itself needs to be updated and information about earlier iteration recorded in a note(s). The current title is recorded in 245 and the title for earlier iterations is recorded in 247 (use Rules 12.7B4.2 and 21.30J).

As mentioned earlier, the implementation of the revised rules was aimed at reducing the number of new records due to title changes. The key role in this intent belongs to the introduction of concepts of 'major' and 'minor' changes, which replaced the concept of 'title change' in Rule 21.2A. According to the revised rule, the new record would be created only when a change in the title proper is major, and no number of minor changes will amount to a major change. The concept of major and minor changes was the result of harmonization of AACR with ISSN and ISBD (CR). The underlying approach in determining whether the change is major or minor is to think whether the change was intended to result in a new work.

The basic breakdown between major and minor changes (summarized in Table 2.5) is as follows.
Major:

- major changes in title;

- changes in corporate body main entry or corporate body uniform title qualifier;

- major change in edition statement;

- physical format.

Minor:

- minor title changes;

- minor change in edition statement;

- minor changes to uniform title qualifier;

- numbering (always minor; result of harmonization with ISSN).

| Table 2.5 | Summary of major and minor changes |

Area of description	Major change (new record)	Minor change (no new record)
Title	First five words (unless minor) After five words if the meaning or scope changed If the corporate body in the title becomes different corporate body	Representation of a word Articles, prepositions Placement and representation of a corporate body in a title Punctuation Order of parallel titles Change in word linking to numbering Change in order of words in a list Change in words indicating type of resource
Corporate body	Change to the corporate body (including uniform title qualifier) Different corporate body Main-entry corporate body no longer responsible	
Edition	Indicates new subject matter Indicates new physical format	Different wording of the same subject matter
Physical format	Change in SMD, e.g. print to online	e.g. HTML to PDF
Numbering		Always minor

Title

Rule 21.2C2 outlines the difference between major and minor title changes. According to the corresponding LCRI, when considering the change always compare it to the title proper (field 245), meaning that any variant titles do not count in the test for a major title change. For a title change to be major, consider any changes to the first five words of the title (six words if the title starts with an article) unless the change is minor. After the first five words the change is considered major if any word changes the meaning of the title or alters the publication's subject matter. If a change to a corporate body which is part of the title indicates that it is a different corporate body, consider this a major title change.[14]

Minor changes to the title include differences in representation of words, e.g. abbreviation versus spelled-out form, even if the change takes place within the first five words of the title; any changes to articles, prepositions and conjunctions; any changes to the name of the same corporate body anywhere in the title; any change in punctuation; change in the order of titles in multiple languages; any changes in the words anywhere in the title that link the title to the numbering; appearance of fluctuating titles; any change in the order of words in a list anywhere in the title, provided there is no change to the subject matter; any changes to the words indicating the type of resource, e.g. *magazine*, *journal*, etc.[15]

Corporate body

Change to the corporate body or a different corporate body constitutes a major change and requires a new record. If the corporate body in a uniform title qualifier changes, consider it a major change, as well as if a corporate body in the main entry is no longer responsible for the publication.[16]

Edition statement

The changes to the edition statement are reflected in LCRI 21.3B, not AACR2. The change is considered major if it indicates change in subject matter or physical format.

Physical format

The same LCRI rule calls for a new record if change takes place in a specific material designation area (fields 007 and 300), for example from print to online. When in doubt, the change is considered minor.

Resource Description and Access

The continuing march of electronic resources and complexities of their issuance and access provision to the contents prompted the JSC to start working on a new standard designed for the digital world. Initially the new rules were called AACR3, but as the work progressed it became clear that a new approach required a new name. So as an outcome of the JSC meeting in April 2005 it was decided to adopt a new working title, Resource Description and Access (RDA).[17] As stated in the RDA prospectus:

> a key element in the design of RDA is its alignment with the conceptual models for bibliographic and authority data developed by the International Federation of Library Associations and Institutions (IFLA). The Functional Requirements for Bibliographic Records and Functional Requirements for Authority Records models provide RDA with an underlying framework that has the scope needed to support comprehensive coverage of all types of content and media, the flexibility and extensibility needed to accommodate newly emerging resource characteristics, and the adaptability needed for the data produced to function within a wide range of technological environments.[18]

Electronic journals in the library setting

By now it is well established that patrons not only prefer but also expect online access to journals rather than the journals in print form. The shift from treating electronic journals as an added convenience to being the default in a user's expectations occurred very quickly, ahead of publishers' ability or willingness to provide online access to their journals. Having a print-only version of the publication has now become almost a disappointment to users. Following patrons' demands and responding to budgets eroded by inflation and real-dollar cuts, libraries are gradually switching to an online-only form of journal delivery.

Production costs of electronic journals are significantly lower and the publishers do not have to concern themselves with such logistics as storage, shipment and handling of the items. Profit margins increased exponentially along with the pace of delivery, consequently publishers favoring the online format employ appropriate price structures to motivate libraries to go online.

Escalating costs aside, it seems that going online is advantageous for both sides. Libraries carry titles without using physical shelf space and please users by providing the preferred form of access; publishers, in their turn, earn hefty profits while satisfying the libraries.

If we examine the situation more closely, however, one notices one group that may be at a disadvantage – the catalogers. By definition, a cataloger's job is to provide access to a library's resources, and when this is not taking place the catalogers are not doing their job. This is a hard pill to swallow for catalogers, who by the nature of their occupation are mostly perfectionists, meticulously creating descriptions, enumerating access points, analyzing subject matter and assigning topic-specific subject headings. All that for the satisfaction of knowing that, thanks to their work, the right resource will be discovered by the user at the right time.

When the first electronic journals emerged, the only challenge for catalogers was to learn the specifics of the new format and the new set of cataloging rules that arose in response to the growing number of electronic periodicals.

At first electronic journals appeared as single publications. They could be original, so-called 'born digital', or duplicate the contents of the print form. Solo journals for a while could be absorbed by catalogers, who, often at the expense of print-form cataloging and due to user preference, made cataloging electronic-format publications their priority. Rapidly, though, the intent of keeping up with the cataloging of emerging e-journals turned into a reaching-the-horizon goal.

When cataloging online journals, each library has to make several decisions in determining local policies on electronic serials. One of the crucial issues every library aspiring to catalog online journals has to resolve is deciding on the type of cataloging treatment: are they going to use a *single-* or *multiple*-record approach?

A single-record approach refers to the type of e-journal cataloging treatment that uses a single bibliographic record to provide access to the print (or any other tangible form) and online forms of the title. A multiple- or separate-record approach refers to the type of cataloging treatment that uses separate bibliographic records to provide access to the print and online forms of the title.

A single-record approach provides more convenience for the user and public services. A multiple-record approach makes it easier for technical services to manipulate data in the catalog, reduces record maintenance and allows more flexibility in terms of collection development. There are pros and cons for each side in this decision. Usually the scale tilts in favor of that argument which carries more weight in a particular library.

Consistency in the catalog has been a steadfast goal of catalogers for a long time. However, as times change this goal has become less attainable and less realistic. The decision regarding the single- or multiple-record approach is a prime example.

At the dawn of the electronic journal era, when publishers had an online version as an add-on to the print one, a great many libraries decided on the single-record approach. It made perfect sense – convenient for the user and relatively easy for catalogers, who could add a few tags to accommodate both versions. The bibliographic utilities, such as the OCLC and RLIN, offered very few online-only records, thus making the option of separate records a domain of original cataloging. In addition, striving for consistency, many libraries with local policies to catalog microfilm and print versions of the resource on a single record interpreted the online form in the same category of materials. But the difference between all previously known forms of publication and the online one manifested itself quickly, the online-only records became abundant and the vendor-produced record sets made single-record approach integration into the catalog extremely cumbersome and ultimately not worth the challenge – and add to that an increasing number of unstable online access sources which made maintenance of the records a never-ending task.

Many libraries recognized that in terms of practicality changing the policy to the multiple-record approach was the only viable option. There is no national policy or recommendation on what approach to use – it is up to each individual library to decide which road to take. The Government Publications Office (GPO) has an established single-record policy. Libraries carrying government documents are most likely to use GPO records and thus have a single-record approach for at least that part of their database. If the library uses single record across the board, GPO records will be consistent with the rest of the catalog. However, if the institution also uses a separate-record approach, inconsistency is inevitable.

It is not suggested here that GPO records should determine the choice of e-journal cataloging policy. The point is that inconsistencies in the catalog may not necessarily be the result of inconsistent policies in the past. With the explosion in the amount of electronic materials to be cataloged and availability of MARC records coming from different sources, inconsistency in the catalog may be the only way to forge ahead. There is nothing wrong or even unusual if a library chose one policy and then had to switch to another. It is better, however, to know in advance the factors that may trigger this change.

In summer 2003, during the World Congress of Library Associations in Berlin, the Section on Serials Publications (later renamed Serials and Other Continuing Resources), where the author has served on the standing committee, organized a panel discussion on e-journal cataloging. Proving the popularity of the topic, the room was packed to capacity. After two hours of heated discussion on how to handle e-journals, Regina Reynolds, head of the National Serials Data Program, did an informal survey of the audience. She asked by show of hands how many libraries used single- and multiple-record approaches.

It is worth noting that for libraries adhering to CONSER policy the preferred treatment has been a single-record approach. Much to the author's surprise, out of the audience of about 150 only three hands responded positively to the single-record option. All of them, including the author, were from American libraries. When the second part of the question came, 'Who is here with the separate-record approach?', a forest of hands arose. It seemed that everyone in the world was using the separate-record approach but the USA. It turned out that other libraries were more concerned about being practical than adhering to the rules. The most-mentioned argument was that if anything changes in the subscription terms or in the journal contents of online aggregators, it would be a snap to get rid of the online records using automatic processes instead of trying to go through every single record manually and edit it.

Another very practical consideration in this issue is integration and maintenance of vendor-provided records if a library uses outside cataloging sources.

Single-record approach

Out of the two choices, the single-record approach is user-friendlier and is usually favored by library patrons. When a library employs this approach, users are taken directly to the record for the title and have access to the description of print and online versions at the same time. In addition, if the library has a note attached to the online address that not only states varying versions of generic 'connect to the online resource' but also specifies the coverage dates, the reader can easily determine the overall compound holdings for the title in the library.

With a single-record approach it is not difficult for the reader to pick the correct record in the title search browse screen – as opposed to a scenario where the search query results in multiple hits displaying different formats of the same title. The confusion is exacerbated when the title index of the catalog includes several forms of title access, e.g. uniform title, title proper, variant title, etc.; multiplied by two, the search may result in up to six hits, with two sets of uniform titles for each format, titles proper and key titles.

In addition to the users, there is convenience in the single-record approach for catalogers as well. It decreases the need for original cataloging of online resources and thus makes cataloging less expensive. Access to the online version is supplied by simple editing of the print record. CONSER Module 31 refers to the single record as a non-cataloging approach and provides editing steps to upgrade the print into a composite record for both forms (Figure 2.8).[19]

There are rare occasions when a library acquires both formats of a publication but the record available from the bibliographic utility is for the online version only. In this case the same set of tags, except for 856, should be applied in relation to the print format to enable the record to provide print access.

Since the single-record approach reduces the number of records in the catalog, there are fewer records to maintain, which is another advantage.

When to use it?

There are several factors to consider when choosing whether to use a single-record approach. First is to ascertain that the

Figure 2.8   Fields needed in print record to include online resource

Code 008/22 ('form of original item') and 008/23 ('form of item') as correct for the original, not for the online version
530 – note availability of online version
740 – Title added entry (or 7xx author/title entry) when the title of the online version differs
856 – Online version location (commonly URL)
776 $t $x – If the online version has a separate ISSN
007 – Optional, computer file characteristics
006 – DO NOT ADD

online version has enough of the same content as the print form and can be considered the same publication. If the online version lacks the full content of the print publication, and provides selective full-text access or supplies abstracts and table of contents only, then the online version may not warrant its own record and should be noted on the print record with an appropriate explanation of the relationship – for example, a note in 856 stating that the link is to the table of contents only.

Another consideration is whether the record for the original version provides adequate access points to accommodate online manifestation. If access points would be different, a single record is not an option. If the content of the online version is fuller than the printed one, and clearly the online version is not a representation of the printed content, then two records, one for each format, will be necessary.

Maintenance is another consideration when choosing a single-record approach. The trend among publishers is that many, while producing two parallel versions of the journal, find it makes more economic sense (profit is what drives most publishers' decisions, not desire to disperse knowledge in every available form) to continue the online format and cease the print version. When this happens, according to LCRI 21.3B, a change of form takes place which requires a new record.

CONSER suggests separate records when the contents of print and online versions differ. However, since the online environment is updated easily and constantly, the contents of the online version may change as the publication progresses and thus in time will be disqualified from residing on the print record as an electronic counterpart.

Practical considerations prevent catalogers from verifying the stability of content in the online version, and so a situation can easily occur when putting the online version on the print record may become misleading and incorrect. If catalogers notice the growing difference between the formats it will necessitate a new record. And thus catalogers are back to where they started, and have to perform redundant work by recataloging the existing record into two versions.

When change of format does occur, it becomes necessary to modify the print record. Any form/title change requires editing the preceding record: closing publication dates, numbering and adding the entry for the succeeding title/form. However, in the case of a record that carried both forms, the cataloger needs to do all the maintenance associated with title change and in addition delete the fields that carried online information: delete 007 if present, delete notes relating to system requirements and transfer the URL links to the new online record or delete them altogether.

Today's catalogers have to follow the rules just like earlier generations, but they also have to take into account the realities of advancing technology. And in the case of the single/separate-record dilemma the reality is such that choosing a single-record approach will make it more difficult to receive record sets from commercial vendors, integrate them and maintain records in the catalog.

In summary, use a single-record approach when:

- print and online versions have the same content and can be considered equivalent;
- print record provides sufficient access points for online version;
- online version lacks full text of the print publication, provides TOC and/or abstracts only and is not worth cataloging separately;

- GPO single record is the only choice for government documents;

- library owns (and will continue to own) both print and online versions of the publication.

Separate-record approach

The advantages and disadvantages of separate-record treatment are opposite to the advantages and disadvantages of the single-record approach.

Advantages include the ability to provide more detailed information about each format; no need to verify and monitor if the content of the online version matches the print format; less maintenance when the title goes online only; clear display of availability of online access in the catalog; less confusion if the library does not own print version but puts online access on the print record; and easier to manipulate data in the catalog and receive, integrate and maintain vendor record sets.

Disadvantages entail confusing multiple hits in the catalog for the same title, split holdings between two formats and a higher number of records to maintain.

With the separate-record approach there are two bibliographic records: one for the original, non-electronic, usually print, version; and the other for the online version. When employing a separate-record approach for the counterparts of a publication, both records carry information about the other form. Figure 2.9 shows the steps to be taken in creating both records.

In summary, use the separate-record approach when:

- full-text online version is not equivalent of the print version;

- more details and access points need to be provided for the online version;

Figure 2.9 Fields needed in separate records for online/ offline counterparts

On the record for the original form (based on combination of CONSER and OCLC rules):

530 – Note availability of online version, e.g. also available via the World Wide Web.

730 – Add title added entry (or 7xx author/title entry) when the title of the online version differs.

776 – Link to the online record in $t [title] and provide e-ISSN in $x – Optional.

856 – Online version location (commonly URL) – Optional.

Create record for the online version using all appropriate fields for the digital form and:

530 – Note the availability of the print form – Optional, e.g. also available in printed form.

730 – Add title added entry (or 7xx author/title entry) when the title of the print version differs.

776 – Link to the print record in $t and provide print ISSN in $x – Optional.

856 – Add location of the electronic version (URL) and $z Public note for the display in OPAC, e.g. $z Connect to the online resource.

- library does not own print form;
- library wants to reduce maintenance when/if the print version ceases or online edition stops being equivalent;
- library considers loading batch records from a vendor.

Aggregator-neutral record

One of the conveniences of the separate-record approach is providing fullness and flexibility in describing the online version. Until 2003 the online record always included the name of the aggregator which provided access to the title. The reality learned by the libraries made it clear that the name of an aggregator is a very unreliable and unstable entry in the catalog record. Journal titles would come and go from the packages or float between the aggregators, and several aggregators can provide access to a journal at the same time.

The last point makes the use of shared cataloging especially challenging and requires extra work in adapting available records to the local catalog. In addition, the whole point of reduced record maintenance in a separate-record approach is defeated by making records outdated every time the aggregator changes or the title separates from an aggregation. Therefore, in 2003 as a result of growing demand from the cataloging community CONSER adopted a policy of an aggregator-neutral record.

The aggregator-neutral record provides for a type of record description that is based on the issuing body, not on an aggregator which provides access to the title. The record is applicable to all variations of online access, whether or not the title has a print counterpart.

In order to create a truly aggregator-neutral record, the name of the provider is kept off the record to the fullest extent. It is not added as a uniform title qualifier, added entry for the corporate name, statement and notes of responsibility or used as a series entry. Any access restrictions or system requirements specific to the aggregator are also excluded from the record.[20]

CONSER policy applies to the journal aggregators, or full-text packages, not the hosts that specialize in article delivery. According to the CONSER guidelines the prioritized list for the sources of the description is as follows.

- The original publisher website when full text is available.

- A host site from an aggregator or archiving site, e.g. JSTOR. Prefer host of an archive site to the publisher site if it contains the first issue and the publisher site does not. Also prefer site that reflects both titles if a title change took place. Beware, however, that a title change from the cataloger's standpoint may not mean the same change for the publisher or the host and vice versa.

■ If access to the online source is not available to the cataloger, base the description on the record for the print version.

■ Article databases that do not maintain issue integrity, e.g InfoTrac.

When creating or adapting an aggregator-neutral record, input information that can be equally applied to different packages. For the original record do not verify information from different sources of the journal to ascertain that data apply to all versions. However, if adapting the record you find that the title entry for the journal in existing records differs from the one you are working on because of the difference in aggregation, provide for the difference by adding variant titles with an explanatory note in $i: 246 1b $i Issues from some providers have title: $a *Title*. Notice that there is no mention of the name of the aggregator in $i.

The only place in the record likely to carry the aggregator name is 856. Unless the web address is universal, for example in government documents or open-access journals, the syntax of URL will most likely contain the name of the provider. In addition, the public note in $z may state the name of the access provider and coverage. Therefore, when accepting a record from the bibliographic utility, examine 856 and notes in $z and edit them to your local requirements if needed. For local needs, libraries can always use local fields for the names of the aggregators to collocate the materials by the provider.

Table 2.6 shows the steps to be taken in creating an aggregator-neutral record.

Table 2.6   Guidelines for aggregator-neutral record creation

008	Code as any online serial.
022	$a electronic ISSN; $y print ISSN.
130/240	Do not use the aggregator's name as a qualifier. Use the print format qualifier as the basis for the online version.
245	Title from the earliest issue available.
246	Added entry if title from multiple providers differs. Use for adapting the record. No need to check multiple title variations when creating an original record. $i Issues from some providers have title: $a *Title*.
260	Name of the place and publisher that is applicable to multiple providers. Do not record digitizer of the name of the aggregator.
362	362 0_ Beginning and ending dates that apply to all online versions, not the coverage from a particular aggregator. 'Coverage as of' notes no longer used (CCM 31.9; LCRI 12.7B10). 362 1_ The beginning date of print version may be given if the first online issue is not accessible or verifiable: 362 1_ Print began with: Vol. 1, no. 1 (Jan. 1985).
4xx, 8xx	Do not use the name of the aggregator or provider as series statement.
500	For the 'Description based on' (if no 362 0_) note construct the appropriate designation taken from the earliest available issue. If not possible, take it from anywhere in the file. Always indicate the source of title proper for the online serial (AACR2 9.7.B3). This is different from the print record, where the source of title proper is given only for the title page substitutes. Use as specific terms as possible, e.g. 'Title from page header'. In parenthesis record the file format, the date when the title was viewed and the version of the access provider used as the basis of description. This is one of the few places where the name of the aggregator/provider may appear in the record. If more than one issue has been used for description, especially when editing the record, give 'latest issue consulted' note with the viewed date in parentheses.
500/550	Do not use aggregator as the publisher or digitizer.

Table 2.6   Guidelines for aggregator-neutral record creation *(Cont'd)*

506	Do not use restrictions note based on aggregator's restrictions. Use the note only if access restrictions apply to all versions, like government-classified documents. Restrictions applied to the aggregators may be noted in $z of 856 field.
538	Mode of access note and system requirement note. Use system requirements note only for unusual requirements applicable to all versions. Also use discretion when applying mode of access note. If mode of access is the World Wide Web, the most common occurrence, and it is evident from other fields in the record, e.g. 856, you may want to skip this field to avoid unnecessary cluttering of the record.
710/730	Use only for corporate bodies that issue the journal and are responsible for its intellectual content. Do not use these fields for the names of the aggregators or providers.
856	Electronic location and access, URL field. Use multiple 856s for each aggregator that the title is available from in your local instance. Keep in mind maintenance issues associated with listing of a volatile source. Unless the resource is an open-access journal or a government document with the URL applicable to all users, this field will always carry local access information. When accepting the record from a bibliographic utility such as the OCLC or RLIN, verify if the existing access link is applicable to your institution and replace it with local form of access if needed. $u is the most commonly used subfield, holding location information of the journal on the internet, the URL. In most ILS this subfield converts the URL into a hotlink in OPAC. $3 is used when the contents of a resource are split among multiple online addresses. This field is used to specify the segment of the resource the 856 is linked to. For example, it can specify the volume range or link to the table of contents. $z is the public display note. In most ILS the wording of this field will be converted into a hotlink absorbing the URL syntax. This note is used widely to indicate the connect instructions, name of the provider and/or associated coverage dates. This is the unique place in the aggregator-neutral record where the name of the aggregator may appear and is necessary to the user for clarification of access.

Issues of access to electronic journals in the library

The biggest challenge libraries face today is providing access to the electronic titles bundled up in aggregator packaging or dispersed in article databases. The traditional approach of creating a MARC record for every title would cost institutions dearly. According to calculations done by the Serials Solutions MARC service, it would cost a library on average $45,625 and 16 months of straight work to catalog 20,000 titles.[21]

Given that Serials Solutions provides the MARC record service, the calculation may be self-serving on its part. However, even if the numbers are somewhat inflated, the cost and investment of time to catalog an e-journal collection fully is exorbitant. Furthermore, creating or even exporting MARC records from the OCLC is only the tip of the iceberg.

Imagine a dream world in which a library had the required resource to catalog titles in every bundle and database. The next biggest hurdle draining the resources of the library will be the maintenance of those records. In addition to the print-era issues associated with a serial record that is never completed, the electronic environment brought additional challenges that might not have been anticipated but manifested themselves promptly.

Serials records have always been notorious for their maintenance requirements long after the title has been cataloged initially. Serials catalogers know all too well that their records are never finished. Title changes, added titles, frequency and designation changes, additional physical forms, ceases, linking fields – all of this and more make serials catalogers go back to the record again and again. In addition to these workings, the online environment introduced such issues as multiple and changeable providers – and corresponding URLs – unstable coverage dates, additions and deletions of the titles from packages. The mere thought of the effort it takes to maintain the accuracy of e-journal records seems daunting. If we take into account the sheer number of online journals available in a medium-size academic library, the job is comparable to the labors of Sisyphus.

Providing access to new forms of material required a novel approach. Traditionally the catalog has been the library's primary tool of access control, but since cataloging and maintaining tens of thousands of titles was not feasible, libraries turned to the internet itself for access to online publications. The most popular alternatives include A–Z lists, home-grown journal databases, content linking and electronic resource management systems.

A–Z lists and databases

A–Z listing is the easiest and a very popular way of providing access to e-journals. A–Z title lists and subject groupings can be created and maintained by the library or produced by an outside vendor. In-house online A–Z lists are easily created by using web-authoring tools, such as DreamWeaver or Contribute, or by employing HTML coding.

The advantage of web lists is their ease of use and low expense of production, or 'the principle of least effort' as applied to librarianship by Chrzastowski.[22] The disadvantages include access to e-journals that is segregated from the tangible library collection; lack of relationship with print counterparts and exclusion of e-journals from the OPAC search results; and limited – if existent at all – searching indexes.

Similar factors apply to e-journal access provided with a database approach. Libraries can store e-journal data in Excel spreadsheets or databases like Access or FileMakerPro to generate webpages from them. This method allows for more sophisticated data manipulation and provides better searching capabilities, depending on the extent of collected data. Along with search and retrieval tools, a database approach can offer A–Z listing of titles, thus presenting an advanced alternative to web lists. The caveat in this approach, however, is the source and relative quality of e-journal data – a weighty consideration if the e-journal database is created and maintained by an outside vendor.

Content linking

Another method of access to e-journals may be provided by embedding links in the content of Abstract & Indexing and full-text article databases. By linking from citations to full text through OpenURL or a DOI (digital object indentifier) link resolver, the user may be guided to an online journal via access to the full-text article. Of course, this will be accidental access. Depending on the database an option may be provided to browse through all available issues of the publication. This method does not give the user a choice of which journal to access and does not provide an opportunity to browse journals through A–Z title or subject lists or search by using specific criteria with an in-house database-access approach, described earlier, including OPAC. However, this database-to-database content linking by way of link resolvers from A&I or hybrid databases to full text is still one method of providing access to electronic journals.

Electronic resource management systems

Electronic resource management (ERM) systems are an emerging powerful tool of accessing online materials, and step in where ILS lack capacity to manage online resources.

The Digital Library Federation identified the functions of ERM systems as 'listing and descriptive'; 'license-related'; 'financial and purchasing'; 'process and status'; 'systems and technical'; 'contact and support'; and 'usage'.[23] ERM systems are capable of providing access to aggregators, article databases and journals on title level. Since ERM systems contain information on titles, holdings, subjects and license agreements, the public display record provides not only links to the resource but also contains its description and an explanation of usage terms. Based on the data contained in ERM systems, libraries can provide title listings or subject groupings of electronic materials.

Why catalog?

The methods of providing access to electronic journals described above can be used separately or in combination. They are by no means mutually exclusive and each has its own advantages. So why catalog e-journals?

Here is a scenario described by Calhoun and Kara:

> 'Does the library subscribe to *Academy of Management Executive*?' This is the sort of question that was once fairly straightforward, but it no longer is. At the time a library user posed this question at Cornell's business school library, the online catalog indicated holdings from 1987 through 1989, and the user left the library shaking his head; he couldn't believe the subscription wasn't current. And guess what: the library does hold an unbroken run. Why wasn't it plain to the user? Because the title was 'buried' in an aggregator database, and the online catalog only reflected print holdings for this title.[24]

Currently there is much discussion about the relevancy of library catalogs. Studies, surveys and plain empirical evidence show that Google and other online engines are the preferred method of accessing information. The principle of least effort is in play again. As pointed out by Marcia Bates, 'users knowingly prefer less reliable information that is easier to find than more reliable information that is harder to discover'.[25]

The problems with current library catalogs were thoroughly analyzed in what became known as the Calhoun Report,[26] in which Karen Calhoun examined the changing role of library catalogs in relation to internet search tools and suggested a plan for 'revitalizing the research library catalog'. The report quickly became controversial and was rejected by many catalogers because one of the suggested strategies for revitalization was to diminish the role of extensive cataloging. As a way of attracting new users to the catalog Calhoun gives the example of the new Endeca catalog at North Carolina State University (www.lib .ncsu.edu/catalog/). This new search engine in the library catalog provides functionalities that weave the capabilities of internet search engines into the richness of the data contained in catalog records.

Another promising trend is the development of such products as Vivisimo (http://vivisimo.com/), which offers clustered search results, and enterprise search engines such as Ex Libris Primo (www.exlibrisgroup.com/webinar_ 1144862525.htm).

There is no question that library catalogs in their current form are fraught with shortcomings. However, today and in the short-term future OPAC will remain the primary instrument for accessing library collections. Over the years libraries have invested millions of dollars in collections that reflect the needs of their local community, support curricula of academic institutions and provide means for student and faculty research – and OPAC has for years been the only tool to navigate these materials. Users came to rely on it so much that they express dismay when unable to search for book, journal and article titles from the single entry point. They certainly expect to see all formats of publications, whether in print or online, in one database. And while OPAC in its current form is unable to provide access at the lowest degree of granularity, such as article-level entries, it should certainly aim at representing a format-comprehensive database. In theory, if MARC records were readily available for article-level entries they could be incorporated in the catalog quite easily.

There are several challenges on the way for this to become a reality: the availability of article-level MARC records and the capabilities of ILS to integrate the records and capacity of MARC data to function as a homogeneous database having diverse levels of granularity. The problem, of course, is that there are not enough article-level MARC records. The other problem is that OPAC can read *only* MARC records, and since many article databases do not use MARC as their metadata standard, AACR2 as the description standard and LCSH as the controlled vocabulary, their records cannot be integrated in the library catalog without extensive massaging of the data. The simpler solution would seem to lie in federated, or meta-, searching by developing crosswalks between different data elements and terminology, and the use of Z39.50 protocol to facilitate searching.

There are many existing crosswalks mapping data between disparate schemata, for example Dublin Core and MARC, or MARC and MODS. However, current ILS do not have the capability of enterprise searching that would allow search engines to walk across data elements within their own domain. If ILS vendors want to stay relevant in the future, this avenue of development is worth pursuing.

While one hopes that the prospect of providing different levels of title access through a single point, whether library catalog or metasearching, will eventually become a reality, we have to provide the best service today with the tools we have at our disposal now. And at this juncture the library catalog remains the primary means to do that.

Libraries should take advantage of the user's awareness of the library catalog and have it work as a one-stop shop. Regardless of the technological acumen of readers, everyone knows about the 'card catalog'. Patrons, even the young ones, who walk into the library looking for one among the computer terminals always surprise the author. The expectation to find the entire spectrum of library materials through the catalog is there, however, and librarians should take advantage of it.

We know that students seek and prefer online access to the print form, often missing out on a library's relevant print resources. Thus by placing access to online electronic journals in the catalog, a library will promote its tangible collection and stimulate systematic scholarship. The Oregon State University Valley Library did a study on search strategies of users; the results showed that students expected to find access to all library materials through the library catalog and not go through different links on the library's homepage.[27] The success of Google and Amazon in large part is based on meeting users' expectations, giving them what they want in simple form, instead of libraries educating and training them in navigation of unfamiliar and complex environments and by doing so sending them back to Google.

In addition to being well positioned to fulfill readers' expectations as a comprehensive resource, a catalog offers advantages that lists and linking-based access do not. Catalog records are created according to data, content and vocabulary standards, thus providing consistent and reliable retrieval. The richness of MARC format allows a catalog to deal with variant changed and related titles, a key feature for serials access.

A catalog contains data on all formats of publication, and thus in the context of print and online journals avoids the problem of split holdings. A catalog also shows continuity of the publication in case of format change. Controlled vocabulary of subject headings allows search, retrieval and collocation by subject, eliminating what Michael Gorman calls 'noise' (the retrieval of irrelevant materials) that comes from relying on keyword searching alone.[28] Prescribed by AACR2, access points existing in MARC records enable users to conduct targeted searches through a variety of catalog indexes. The experience of the University of Tennessee at Knoxville, shared in an article fittingly entitled 'Report of the death of the catalog is greatly exaggerated', showed a twofold increase in usage statistics for electronic journals once their bibliographic records were added to the catalog.[29] And let us not forget authority control, a behind-the-scenes identification and collocation device still unattainable in commercial search engines.

In real life, however, the prevalent reason for libraries opting out of cataloging e-journals is an insurmountable increase in the workload and not underappreciation of bibliographic access. Once the library decides to catalog its e-journal collection, it faces an uphill battle in several directions.

Numbers

If a medium-size academic library has been steadily adding full-text aggregators to its collection for the past few years, with the proliferation of online publications and transformation of print journals into electronic ones the collection of online periodicals could grow from zero to

25,000 in just a few years. This growth is in addition to standard expansion of tangible resources. Let us say that on average it takes about ten minutes to find and copy-catalog a record for an e-journal. This means it will take 250,000 minutes, or 520 days of full-time work, to catalog an average e-journal collection, assuming that every title will have a record available from a shared cataloging utility. Meantime the library is paying for subscriptions and cannot afford to delay access in order to catalog the resources. The cost of cataloging, of course, also makes cataloging large electronic serials collections prohibitive. Despite the efforts of shared cataloging, many e-journal titles do not have an OCLC record and require original cataloging.

According to a study by Colorado State Publications Library, the cost of original cataloging of electronic resources is $58.72 per record.[30] Depending on the percentage of original cataloging in the electronic collection, cataloging large numbers of online journals contained in aggregators and article databases becomes not only very slow but also a very expensive process.

Lack of guidance

Cataloging is infamous, or famous – depending on your vantage point – for its sticky adherence to the standards. Some of us obsess over punctuation, spacing and implementation of every obscure rule while creating MARC records. Unbeknownst to the outside world, standards make our lives easier and the lack thereof leaves us at a loss. This is precisely why cataloging electronic journals is no easy feat. There is no single established national standard and uniform practice for such a task. AACR2's attempts to catch up with electronic reality brought about revision of Chapters 9 and 12 in 2002. This was a necessary but incomplete solution, since AACR2 was never intended for digital materials, and thus the revisions serve only as a temporary band-aid for the lack of a comprehensive e-cataloging policy.

The new RDA is envisioned as a radical change in the approach to electronic resources. It will be the first cataloging standard designed specifically for the digital environment, and is supposed to remedy the confusion of electronic resource catalogers. But the new standard is still at a developmental stage and is a few years away from implementation. MARC adjusted to online materials by introducing the 856 field that underwent a series of coding changes, and its usage is still open to interpretation. CONSER acted by introducing Module 31 for online serials. However, some key elements are in the form of recommendations and many decisions are optional. Moreover, opting for a single-record approach goes against AACR2 rules that require separate records for different formats.

The duality of confusion stems on the one hand from the lack of a clear national standard for cataloging online resources; on the other hand there may be too many standards that can be applied to e-journal cataloging. In addition to the abovementioned AACR2 and CONSER, there are also LC guidelines, LCRI for cataloging and coding internet resources and OCLC guidance.[31] With this array of rules and guidelines, vague national policy and unclear terminology (no clear definitions of the types of electronic resources are currently available), it is up to an individual library that decides to go into the business of cataloging e-journals to establish local policies and procedures and define best practices. As noted in a survey by the Cataloging Electronic Resources/Electronic Resource Display in OPAC (CatER) Task Force of the Illinois Library Computer Systems Organization (ILCSO) Users' Advisory Group, many libraries do not even use standards as absolute authority but more as 'field by field guidance'.[32] Developing and documenting local cataloging guidelines and best practices require a substantial investment of staff and time resources. And similar to the serial record itself, these documents are bound to be infinite work-in-progress as the digital landscape constantly changes and new cataloging standards emerge.

Maintenance

Cataloging by itself is only the first step in providing access to electronic journals. Without records' upkeep the library database will be frozen in time and present a snapshot of a one-time state of affairs. Maintenance of the catalog records, however, is the most time-consuming task and another reason why libraries opt out of cataloging online journal collections.

There are several reasons why maintaining access to online journals is particularly challenging. One reason has to do with the nature of serials in general but is even more pronounced in the context of electronic journals: online journals change titles and get new alternate titles; some changes are major and require a new record and inter-record linking; some are minor and the existing record can be amended with less effort.

What is happening more frequently is a format change from print to online. If an online journal was not born digital then it first appeared as a companion format of a print journal. Most likely, your library noted its existence on the print record. As more and more journals switch to online only, discontinuing print format, the old record needs to be closed and the new one for the electronic format created. It is safe to assume that format change triggering a closure of the print record and creation of the new one for the online version happens more often than title changes and ceases in 'traditional' journals.

The other maintenance issue has to do not with bibliographic control but rather with technical, access-related aspects. There are two scenarios here. The first occurs when a library has direct access to the journal, meaning it has a subscription through the publisher. In this case if anything alters in the publisher's URL, for example the actual publisher changes or the publisher switches publication hosting services (platforms), it will by extension trigger a change in the journal's internet address. Some publishers notify customers about the change, but many do not. The ways in which libraries find out about the changes range from readers' alerts to running URL-checking software provided by some ILS.

Another scenario involves a complex aggregator package environment. If an aggregator provides a library's access to a journal, the library is completely excluded from communication with the publisher and deals with the publisher's surrogate, i.e. the aggregator. Communication between the aggregator and the publisher takes place out of sight of the library and the library is left to deal with the end result of this communication. What is more, the aggregator itself adds another level of complexity by dictating and changing the terms of access to the entire package.

Aggregations

The challenges of access to a single journal also apply to aggregators, but the sheer volume of titles contained in an aggregation compounds the problem. Additional difficulties stem from the nature of the aggregation. When titles are added and taken away on a monthly, if not weekly, basis, catalogers have to roll with the punches. Someone in the library has to keep track of the aggregator titles and edit records depending on the situation. If a title is dropped from an aggregation, or the subscription to the entire package is cancelled, the record needs to be suppressed or deleted (although considering the volatility of aggregations – titles not only disappear but emerge as well – it may be wiser just to suppress the record in case the title reappears with the same aggregator a while later, or gets added to another package).

If a journal changes aggregator, the corresponding URL has to be updated; if a journal becomes available from an additional aggregator, another URL has to be added to the record, especially if the access thresholds differ; if an aggregator adds a new journal, a bibliographic record for the new title needs to be created. And consider this 'reduced' maintenance, presuming that the library adopted the aggregator-neutral record approach!

Acquisitions

Besides strictly bibliographic reasons for the volatility of electronic journals, there is also an acquisitions aspect of the matter. Many publishers began providing electronic versions of their journals as a free add-on to the print subscriptions. As users' preferences changed in favor of online access, the electronic form became a preferred type of publication, and free access often morphed into an add-on charge. If this change is not caught on time, the journal access will lapse. Interruption in subscription to an electronic title will be evident quicker than a print one and the library has to act swiftly. In the words of Wittenbach, 'at this point, the decision needs to be made, in collaboration with bibliographers, whether to pay for and reinstate online access, go with print-only access, or even choose online-only access, if it's available'.[33]

Communication with the various vendors is carried out primarily by acquisitions staff, thus their role in conveying changes of access to catalogers is essential.

Technology

In addition to the issues of bibliographic and acquisitions maintenance, a big part of access sustainability belongs to technology. Remote access to electronic journals is all but expected service today, especially for academic and research libraries. In order to provide off-campus access to resources, the library has to put a substantial effort into maintaining the proxy server and developing and maintaining methods of patrons' authentication. The difficulty of this aspect in journal accessibility was cited in a survey conducted by the CatER Task Force.[34] While this problem would equally apply to OPAC records as well as web lists, it has a compound effect for the library considering cataloging individual titles.

Staffing

Closely related and stemming from the problems described above, a major concern when deciding whether to catalog electronic journals is adequate staffing. In a 1999 survey conducted by the University of Nebraska at Lincoln, 44 per cent of respondents cited insufficient time and staff as the main reasons why they did not provide access to e-journals via OPAC.[35] In 2002 Duranceau conducted a staffing survey testing a hypothesis that the problem of staffing for e-resources has reached a critical level.[36] The results showed that in a five-year period 'staff at least doubled (100 percent increase), but collections grew at least ten times larger in the same period (1,000 percent)'. She points out:

> while libraries have been adding staff in response to needs for e-resource support, they have not been adding staff in a way that comes close to being in proportion to collection growth. While one would not expect or even need staff and collections to have grown in exact proportion to each other, the fact that staff and collection growth are an order of magnitude apart does strongly suggest that more staff needs to be deployed in e-collection support.
>
> Addressing the staffing for e-journals cataloging, the survey revealed that 14 of the 15 libraries responding to the survey indicated that they have staff involved in cataloging e-resources. In all but one case the potentially highly labor-intensive work of representing e-resources in OPACs has been handled through reassignment and/or the addition of duties to current workloads.[37]

The same problem was cited in the CatER study: a lack of 'time to train staff, write documentation, update the records'.[38] Both surveys showed that with budgetary constrains and frequent cutbacks, most libraries approach the staffing problem by reorganizing workflow and reassigning vacant positions, not adding new employees.

In addition to staff numbers, there is an issue of staff qualifications. As Wittenbach points out, libraries are finding that acquisition and processing of e-journals involve more staff and time and a higher staff skill level than for their print counterparts.[39] Staff involved in providing access to electronic resources need to be more technologically oriented and fast learners, as technology marches forward and presents new challenges on a daily basis.

In an article presenting the viewpoints of some professionals in the field, Collins describes the evolving role of the serials cataloger as becoming more technical as serials continue to move to electronic form.[40] Reflecting this development, she points out the evolution of the job title as well, giving examples of the new-generation nomenclature, such as digital production unit head (Terry Reese, Oregon State University) and serials access librarian (Steve Shadle, University of Washington). 'Both of these positions are examples of the potential future for serials catalogers highlighting either programming or workflow management expertise.'[41]

Subscribers to the library listserves can observe this dynamic in real time through the postings on the SERIALIST and AUTOCAT listserves, which increasingly advertise for positions of electronic resources librarian, electronic serials specialist, etc. This is not to say that the time-honored responsibilities of the serials cataloger became obsolete; it is more of an indication that the online environment has forced catalogers to acquire new skills, enabling them to perform their traditional duties in a new library environment.

Lease versus own

Some librarians have a philosophical dilemma over whether e-journal titles 'deserve' to be cataloged. As opposed to print journals, whose past contents the library owns whether or not the subscription has been cancelled or title ceased, the content of online journals is leased and often is available only so long as the library currently pays the subscription, the journal is in publication and/or the aggregator has it as part of the package. Such an ephemeral nature of access to e-journals may not justify efforts to catalog them.

The question of permanent access to back volumes has been a contentious issue between libraries and publishers since the dawn of the electronic era. Some providers, like JSTOR, allow perpetual access to the paid contents and some offer access to back files with a current subscription. Nevertheless, the prevailing fluid nature of access to e-journals and lack of option for archiving the content paid for in the past may be a serious consideration in deciding whether to catalog an online journal collection. Some libraries solve this problem by cataloging individual journals only from stable aggregators, such as JSTOR and Project Muse. In the CatER survey, 46 per cent of respondents considered the key factor for cataloging 'that these journals, once purchased, remain permanently a part of the library's holdings regardless of whether the subscription remains current; additionally, the URLs tend to remain static'.[42]

The addressed issues clearly demonstrate that adding electronic journals to the catalog is beset with various pitfalls. The sheer volume of the journals notwithstanding, the biggest problem is presented by the aggregations that contain the majority of a library's electronic journal collection.

Notes

1   *Anglo-American Cataloguing Rules, Second Edition, 2002 Revision (AACR2R).* Ottawa and Chicago: Canadian Library Association/American Library Association.
2   Ibid.
3   Ibid.
4   Hirons, Jean and Graham, Crystal (1998) 'Issues related to seriality', in *The Principles and Future of AACR*, proceedings of International Conference on Principles and Future Development of AACR, Toronto, Ontario,

23–25 October 1997. Ottawa and Chicago: Canadian Library Association/American Library Association; available at: *http://epe.lac-bac.gc.ca/100/200/300/jsc_ aacr/issues/r-serial.pdf* (accessed: 17 February 2007).

5 Available at: *www.collectionscanada.ca/jsc/docs/ser- rep.pdf* (accessed: 17 February 2007).

6 Available at: *www.ifla.org/VII/s13/frbr/frbr.pdf* (accessed: 17 February 2007).

7 *AACR2R*, note 1 above, Appendix D, Glossary.

8 Ibid.

9 Ibid.

10 Ibid.

11 *AACR2R*, note 1 above.

12 Ibid., Appendix D, Glossary.

13 Tillett, Barbara (2002) 'LC implementation of 2002 revision of AACR2', 1 December; available at: *www.loc.gov/catdir/pcc/ir/AACR2rev_ovrvbt02_files/ v3_document.htm* (accessed: 17 February 2007).

14 *AACR2R*, note 1 above, Revision 21.2C2a.

15 Ibid., Revision 21.2C2b.

16 Ibid., Revision 21.3B1.

17 Available at: *www.collectionscanada.ca/jsc/0504out .html* (accessed: 17 February 2007).

18 Available at: *www.collectionscanada.ca/jsc/rdaprospectus .html* (accessed: 17 February 2007).

19 CONSER Module 31.2.3; available at: *www.loc.gov/ acq/conser/Module31.pdf* (accessed: 17 February 2007).

20 CONSER Module 31.

21 Available at: *http://serialssolutions.com/marccalculator .asp* (accessed: 17 February 2007).

22 Chrzastowski, T.E. (1999) 'E-journal access: the online catalog (856 field), web lists, and the principle of least effort', *Library Computing Westport*, 18(4): 317–22.

23 Jewell, Timothy D. (2002) *Selection and Presentation of Commercially Available Electronic Resources.* Washington, DC: Digital Library Federation and Council on Library and Information Resources; available at: *www.clir.org/pubs/reports/pub99/pub99 .pdf* (accessed: 17 February 2007).

24 Calhoun, Karen and Kara, Bill (2000) 'Aggregation or aggravation? Optimizing access to full-text journals', *ALCTS Newsletter Online*, 11(1); available at: *http://archive.ala.org/alcts/alcts_news/v11n2/gateway_ pap15.html* (accessed: 19 November 2006).

25 Bates, Marcia J. (2003) 'Improving user access to library catalog and portal information: final report', prepared for Library of Congress, Section 2A, 'General information seeking behavior'; available at: *www.loc.gov/catdir/bibcontrol/2.3BatesReport6- 03.doc.pdf* (accessed: 19 November 2006).

26 Calhoun, Karen (2006) *The Changing Nature of the Catalog and its Integration with Other Discovery.* Washington, DC: Library of Congress, 17 March; available at: *www.loc.gov/catdir/calhoun-report- final.pdf* (accessed: 17 February 2007).

27 Banerjee, Kyle (2000) 'Challenges of using metadata in a library setting: the Collection and Management of Electronic Links (CAMEL) project at Oregon State University', *Library Collections, Acquisitions, & Technical Services*, 24(2): 217–27.

28 Hinton, Melissa J. (2001) 'On cataloging internet resources: voices from the field', *Journal of Internet Cataloging*, 5(1): 53–67.

29 Johnson, Kay, Manoff, Maribeth and Sheffield, Rebecca (2003) 'Report of the death of the catalog is greatly exaggerated: the e-journal access journey at the University of Tennessee', *Serials Librarian*, 44(3/4): 285–93.

30 Available at: *www.cde.state.co.us/stateinfo/download/ pdf/December_2004.pdf* (accessed: 9 July 2006).

31 *Bibliographic Formats and Standards and Cataloging Internet Resources – A Manual and Practical Guide*; available at: *www.oclc.org/support/documentation/ worldcat/cataloging/electronicresources/* (accessed: 17 February 2007).

32 Chen, Xiaotian, Colgan, Larry, Greene, Courtney, Lowe, Elizabeth and Winke, Conrad (2004) 'E-resource cataloging practices: A survey of academic libraries and consortia', *Serials Librarian*, 47(1/2): 153–79.

33 Wittenbach, Stefanie (2003) 'Everything you always wanted to know about electronic journals but were afraid to ask', *Serials Librarian*, 44(1/2): 14.

34 Chen et al., note 32 above.

35 Martin, Charity K. (2002) 'Do we catalog or not? How research libraries provide bibliographic access to electronic journals in aggregated databases', *Serials Librarian*, 43(1): 61–77.

36 Duranceau, Ellen Finnie (2002) 'Staffing for electronic resource management: the results of a survey', *Serials Review*, 28(4): 316–20.

37 Ibid.

38 Chen et al., note 32 above.

39 Wittenbach, note 33 above.

40 Collins, Maria H. (2005) 'The effects of e-journal management tools and services on serials cataloging', *Serials Review*, 31(4): 291–7.

41 Ibid.

42 Chen et al., note 32 above.

3

Aggregators

What is an aggregator and what does it aggregate? The answer, in library-speak, is that an aggregator creates an aggregation, or a package of electronic publications.

There are different types of aggregators, which may bring confusion into this common library term. Inger delineates three classes of aggregators. Firstly, there are companies whose primary focus is to provide a hosting service for publishers – the content host. Secondly, there are those which index or categorize disparate content on other content host services – the gateways. And lastly, there are the 'traditional aggregators of licensed full text content – the full text aggregators'.[1]

Calhoun and Kara categorize the product of aggregators – aggregations – in a similar vein:

> Some of the more common types of aggregations are those that are collections of titles by one publisher or based on a broad subject. Publisher-based aggregations are those in which all the journals in the collection are from one publisher. Subject-based aggregations are those that can include publications from numerous publishers but are related in that they share the same broad subject, whether business, medicine/health, law, literature, etc., or whether they're meant to serve as a broad general periodicals

collection. In addition, full-text publications can be accessed through vendors who have aggregated the journals of many publishers and make them available through their services.[2]

Martin and Hoffman define the aggregator as a vendor or publisher which gathers the content (usually full text) of dozens to thousands of serials titles and makes them available to a subscribing institution; an aggregated database is a collection of electronic resources from separately issued publications, assembled as a convenience to libraries and other subscribing institutions.[3]

In his 2002 white paper commissioned by NISO, *The Exchange of Serials Subscription Information*, Ed Jones defines an aggregation service as an agency offering packages of content (aggregations) – usually subject-oriented with associated indexing – that may include the abstracts and full text of the indexed items. Access to the full text of publications in aggregations is typically included in the cost of subscribing to the aggregation and is independent of any subscription to the underlying publication. The publications included in an aggregation may change over the course of a given subscription to that aggregation as publications are added and dropped, and individual publications may be subject to embargoes on access to recent content in order to encourage separate subscriptions to the publications involved. Examples are Gale, ProQuest and EBSCOhost.[4]

And according to CONSER, an aggregator is:

a company that provides digitized access to the content of many different serials and other resources, often from a variety of different publishers. Aggregators may also be called by other terms, including but not limited to:

distributors, vendors, or secondary publishers. Aggregators provide access to digitized material through a searchable database. Generally the collections that aggregators produce fall into two different categories: those that provide access to complete issues of serials and those that contain the text of selected articles from serial issues.[5]

Aggregated databases are both a blessing and a curse. They are a blessing for collection development and acquisitions, as well as patrons; and a curse for catalogers struggling to provide access to the journals contained in the aggregations.

Blessing

By subscribing to a subject aggregation, bibliographers receive a package of titles germane to the discipline that they would otherwise have to pick one by one and evaluate. A tremendous effort would have to be made to discover journals and keep abreast with new ones. Subscribing to a journal database from a reputable aggregator elevates the evaluation process from the title to the collection level. In addition, acquiring a substantial number of titles at once provides a library with instant coverage of a subject. Price-wise, paying in volume to the aggregators is often cheaper than buying journals separately. Of course, an all-or-nothing approach in subscribing to those databases is frustrating and often, mainly because of budgetary considerations, libraries are forced to choose 'nothing'.

The light in the tunnel here is that aggregators are for-profit businesses and by definition have to be sensitive to market conditions. The 'nothing' response does not benefit vendors either, so they constantly develop new pricing models, now more frequently offering subsets of big and expensive collections that are more affordable and aim at a smaller segment of subject coverage.

For acquisitions staff, dealing with one e-journal aggregator instead of hundreds of separate publishers is similar to the situation with the print form. An aggregator in this context acts as a counterpart to a print subscription agent. Acquisitions have to pay only one invoice, not hundreds, and renew only one subscription. In the case of cancelling a subscription, it is only one order to close. The same applies to negotiating licensing terms and coverage data.

Patrons benefit from aggregator databases by gaining online access to hundreds of titles at once, especially valuable in subject aggregations. In addition, aggregators supply more stable URLs and OpenURLs that enable use of linking technologies. Very important for the user is an aggregator's common interface that permits searching across all journals simultaneously, and universal subject headings, descriptor terms and thesauri, the trademarks of controlled vocabularies that allow reliable searching, retrieval and collocation.

Curse

Yes, catalogers should be vicariously happy for collection development and acquisitions. And they do have satisfaction of user needs and wants as their primary objective. However, they are the ones who carry the burden of providing access to the materials to satisfy those needs (assuming the library wants to catalog electronic journals).

When aggregator databases first emerged on the scene, the natural reaction of catalogers was to catalog every title. And they did. The author remembers when the first aggregation appeared at the Getty Research Library – it was Project Muse, Arts and Humanities Collection. At the time the package was around 200 titles. The load was split between two serials catalogers, and the job was done in a week. A single-record approach was used if the title had a print version, and most born-digital journals had records in the RLIN database. It was the easiest cataloging the author had ever done. It all was so straightforward – titles stayed intact, coverage dates were stable, and all that with the convenience of online access. Then the library acquired more aggregations with more titles. Catalogers tried to stay afloat, dividing workflow.

What happened next is all too familiar to any serials cataloging unit that is trying to do its job. It felt like the first aggregations were scattered warm raindrops, which we enjoyed; then it started raining harder and we held up umbrellas trying to stay dry; then it poured – and we gave up trying to stay dry and ran inside. And we are still there.

To illustrate the explosion in the growth rate of e-journals, here are some numbers. At the dawn of the electronic era in 1991, the *Chronicle of Higher Education* reported six peer-reviewed electronic journals.[6] The ARL *Directory of Scholarly Electronic Journal and Academic Discussion Lists, 2000* contains over 3,900 peer-reviewed e-journal titles.[7] In a ten-year period, the number of peer-reviewed electronic journals had grown by over 65,000 per cent! In October 2000 *Ulrich's International Periodicals Directory* (www.ulrichsweb.com/UlrichsWeb/) listed 20,430 active serials available 'exclusively online' or in addition to a print counterpart.[8] Five years later, in 2005, the author ran a search at Ulrich looking for online journals and came back with a staggering 43,985 results; and according to some electronic journal subscription management services, the 2007 number will easily double that.

What is the problem?

Presuming a library decides to catalog aggregations on a journal title level, the scenario will present catalogers with two major problems: contents and access. Contents has to do with maintenance of the package's titles, multiplied by the overall number of aggregated databases to which the library subscribes. Access is related to cataloging and maintenance of the e-journal records.

Contents

Aggregator packages are notoriously unstable. The titles come and go, coverage dates change depending on the contract with the publishers or, in a consortia environment, depending on the agreement between the consortium and an aggregator. Those deals often change, resulting in titles disappearing from the package or new journals appearing.

Access

Access problems in aggregations are related to the fluid nature of serials in general, as well as e-journal-specific issues. The general problems pertain to title changes, merges and ceases and apply to any type of serial, whether print or electronic. With electronic journals, however, it is difficult to catch the change since most libraries do not check them in. One e-journal catalog record can have several links to different aggregators, each with different coverage depending on the specific agreement of the publisher with each aggregator.

If the library does not subscribe to commercial e-journal management programs, keeping track of those changes across all aggregations in the library is extremely time-consuming and impractical. Many publishers offer notification and alert services either on their websites or through e-mail. But even keeping track of the alerts and following up on them is very time-consuming. If the subscription is cancelled with an aggregator, the corresponding links need to be deleted from the record, or if the source of access was a single aggregator the entire record needs to be deleted or suppressed.

Considering the other side of volatility of aggregators – that titles not only go but come as well – it may be wiser to suppress the record and not delete it in case the title reappears in the same aggregator a while later, or emerges in another package.

In 2003 TDNet, a library electronic resources management company, conducted a project measuring changes in URL, title coverage and coverage dates at the University of Michigan (UM) and the University of Nebraska at Lincoln (UNL).[9] They gathered weekly changes for 18 months at UNL and six months at UM. Non-URL changes included title, coverage, publisher, ISSN, e-ISSN and aggregator changes. UNL had 24,090 serials titles: during the project period 14,680 titles were added via the aggregators and 170 titles added individually. Non-URL changes in aggregators included 3,592 deleted titles and 20,491 other changes. Combined with URL changes, there were a total of 40,060 changes. UM had 19,667 titles: during the six-month period there were 1,511 added titles in aggregators, 1,342 deleted titles and 5,544 other changes. Combined with URL changes there were a total of 9,366 changes.

As you can see, manual title and record maintenance in an aggregator environment is an unaffordable and counterproductive time drain for catalogers. So libraries, even those striving for their catalog to be a one-stop shop, have to choose between best access and some access – in favor of some access, i.e. linking to e-journals through an aggregator A–Z title and/or subject list.

Growth and volatility of aggregated packages increase exponentially and many libraries realize that they cannot do it alone. Like never before, libraries have to turn for help to commercial companies for at least some kind of electronic journal management assistance.

Commercial options

Obtaining MARC records from commercial services has been an option for libraries for quite some time. For some companies automation of library cataloging is the primary focus, others provide MARC record sets as a value-added product to their publishing or bookselling services and yet a third type includes providers of library technology. Companies in the first category include The Library Corporation (TLC), MARCIVE and PromptCat (a cataloging arm of the OCLC). (If a library is an OCLC subscriber, keep in mind that PromptCat, in addition to MARC record delivery, offers concurrent activation of holdings in the OCLC, releasing the library from this additional workflow step.) Libraries can either contract these companies directly or acquire records as part of their ordering and subscription operations with participating partners, e.g. The Book House, Baker & Taylor and recently Amazon. Companies where library cataloging services are piggybacked to their main business, such as Thomson-Gale and EBSCO, may offer free MARC records tied to acquired titles and packages. Yet another source of MARC records includes ILS companies, such as Ex Libris (just bought by Francisco Partners) and its record-providing MARCit service.

It was noted earlier that cataloging electronic journals solves only one of the problems of e-journal access. Even if a library takes advantage of vendor-provided record sets to enable it instantly to put on the map hundreds, if not thousands, of titles, a bigger challenge is still ahead: keeping information about this access current. To answer this challenge by combining two major components of electronic journal management – cataloging and continuous maintenance – a new type of service emerged on the library market.

Ed Jones, in his 2002 white paper, formulated a definition for this type of service and coined a now widely accepted term, PAMS (publication access management service), meaning an agency offering customers basic and updated data on the publications to which they have access rights, whether these publications are hosted locally or remotely. The data may be used to update a variety of local systems, including local management tools, local e-publication webpages and records in the local catalog. Examples are jake, Serials Solutions and TDNet.[10]

Jake (jointly administered knowledge environment) from Yale University is now defunct. The database is still online (http://jake.med.yale.edu/index.jsp), but it has not been updated since 2002. Commercially available e-journal managers at one time included Journal Web Cite and Serials Cybrarian, but these are no longer in business (Journal Web Cite was bought by TDNet in 2003), so the remaining major players on the PAMS market now are Serials Solutions and TDNet.

Serials Solutions

Serials Solutions is a company founded by a librarian for librarians.[11] Peter McCracken conceived the idea while working as reference librarian at the University of Washington, Seattle. Frustrated by the lack of tools to manage electronic periodicals, in 2000 McCracken, his two brothers Steve and Mike and their friends Chris Pierard and Tim Granquist co-founded Serials Solutions, a web-based solution to assist librarians with e-journal management problems.[12]

The first product it offered in 2000 was an electronic journals title list. Its next goal was to provide enhanced access to the titles in database aggregations through OPAC. As Peter McCracken himself wrote: 'While it was not possible when the company began, the development of extensive internal technology and software now allows Serials Solutions to combine the heart of the title lists – the background data – with quality MARC records from the CONSER database.'[13] The launch of a full MARC record service in 2001 made Serials Solutions the first electronic journal management company to offer such a service. In 2004 the company was purchased by ProQuest.[14]

Currently it tracks 107,800 unique titles from 1,317 full-text databases (most are aggregated) from 455 content providers. Orlo Willis of Serials Solutions indicated that the system shows some duplication, so in their best estimate it manages around 70,000 truly unique titles.[15] Serials Solutions provides such services as:

- Central Search (federated searching);
- Article Linker (OpenURL resolver);
- MARC records;
- Access and Management Suite (AMS);
- electronic resource management system.

TDNet

TDNet was founded in 1998 by Asher Sofrin and Aliza Friedman, then chief executive and marketing manager respectively at Teldan Information Systems, the most prominent domestic library supplier and information provider in Israel. The impetus for the company was the realization that it was becoming more and more difficult for libraries to manage their growing electronic journal collections. The international launch of the company was held in 2000 at the IFLA conference in Jerusalem. In 2001 TDNet was incorporated in the USA with Michael Markwith as president.[16] TDNet offers an *à la carte* solution for e-journal management. Its Resource Manager service includes:

- Searcher Analyzer (federated searching);
- Journal Manager (access, weekly updates, statistics for e-journal collections);
- TOUR Resolver (OpenURL resolver);
- Holdings Manager (MARC records).

TDNet currently manages over 90,000 unique electronic journals and 600 aggregated databases,[17] and is the only serials management company that offers a TOC alerting service.

Comparing services

In 2002 Sitko et al.[18] and Duranceau[19] offered a detailed comparison of the two companies. At the time TDNet was considered a more comprehensive service with a wider array of e-journal management tools, such as title-level access, statistics, subject searching and TOC alerts. Serials Solutions' corporate strategy was to focus mainly on e-journal title lists, and among its service shortcomings were a lack of statistical reports, infrequent data updates, no choice between the local or vendor's server and package-level links. However, the company went a long way to catch up with its competition and earn recognition among the library community.

Serials Solutions now offers an analogous range of services (except for TOC alerts, which remain TDNet's prerogative). In addition, at least for now, only Serials Solutions offers an ERM system. Pricing models in both services are based on the number of titles they track for the client. Libraries may expect a higher dollar output for the TDNet services, a fact the company gently alludes to on its website describing its suite of electronic journal management services. Resource Manager is 'a solution to access and management of paid-for and of free-on-the-web resources. It reflects users' references while respecting access arrangements of the institution and the enterprise. Compared to competitors it adds more value to librarians and to information users; the extra value comes at a fraction of the nominal cost and of the overall cost-to-operate of other solutions.'[20] However, as Sitko et al. pointed out, 'for some libraries, the cost of TDNet will be unaffordable regardless of the valuable and unique features'.[21]

In comparing itself with TDNet, Orlo Willis of Serials Solutions points out:

> the primary difference between Serials Solutions and TDNet is the value we add to the raw publisher data. From what I understand, TDNet collects the holdings data from the content providers and essentially passes it through unaltered. Serials Solutions, on the other hand, performs a number of steps designed to add value to that raw publisher data. Some of the things we do include:
>
> - Comparison between this update and the last update to see what has changed
> - Normalization (associating the titles with the appropriate CONSER record) which allows us to standardize the way titles are displayed and also

attach a plethora of other metadata to the journal record

- Subject classifications
- Alternate title representations and searching
- Publisher
- Associations with other media types such as electronic, microform, CD
- Automated rule application which allows us to make changes to holdings information that comes in consistently wrong from the content providers, i.e. incorrect ISSN, incorrect date range, etc. This functionality also allows us to add title splits (previous or subsequent versions of a title) that are not represented by the content provider.

I'm sure there's more but the main thing is that we have a whole team of people whose job it is to audit the holdings data on a continual basis. This human element in tandem with our proprietary tools is what makes the difference.[22]

PAMS offers a menu of services that libraries can pick and choose from or use in ensemble. When engaging PAMS services libraries need to define their goals and match them against vendors' products. As Michael Gorman suggested in his third 'new library law', technology must be used intelligently to enhance service – and used when it is useful, affordable and cost-effective.[23] What kind of services would be needed to achieve all or some of the library's goals? They include some of the following (Table 3.1):

- enumerate electronic journals dispersed throughout the aggregator databases;
- enumerate 'single' journals, or journals outside aggregator databases;

Table 3.1 Summary of library goals and matching PAMS services

Library goal	Matching commercial service
Title list of full-text electronic journals available through aggregator databases	Title list service
Title list of singe journals	Title list service
Accurate coverage dates	Holdings service
Collocation by aggregator/hosting service/publisher	Title list service or MARC record service with a designated field for provider's name
'One-stop shop' for library collections	MARC record service
Searching across multiple databases	Federated searching or metasearching
Usage statistics and title overlap analysis	Statistical reports service
Citation to full text linking	OpenURL, DOI link resolvers
License, subscription and access management tool	Electronic resource management (ERM) system

- collocate journals by aggregator/hosting service/publisher;
- provide one-point access to the library collection, including monographs, serials holdings in all formats and integrated resources;
- search across multiple article databases;
- link a citation to the full text of the article;
- perform statistical and overlap analysis;
- provide a centralized system for license, subscription and access management.

How do they know?

One of the first questions a library not yet using PAMS services will ask is how do 'they' know? Who are the parties involved in data exchange and what kind of information flow and communication trajectories take place for the services to work?

Ed Jones outlined a detailed analysis of these communications in his white paper.[24] The purpose of Jones's analysis was to identify current and potential applications in which serials subscription data are exchanged; identify the formats currently in use for such exchange; and ascertain the perceived utility of standards to support the exchange, including standard identifiers for subscribers and services. To stay within its scope, this book will examine the conclusions relevant only to the paper's first objective: current information flows in which serials subscription data are exchanged.

The end result of the process allows a user to find an electronic journal in the library, whether via OPAC or through an online A–Z list, and data about the journal, including accurate coverage dates. All this involves information exchange between libraries, publishers, hosting services, subscription agents and PAMS.

- Publishers communicate to hosting services and aggregators bibliographic data about the titles.

- Publishers, hosting services and aggregators inform PAMS about the titles they include in their e-journal collections:

  - publishers/hosting services to PAMS include:
    - publisher/hosting service
    - title
    - ISSN
    - start date
    - end date
    - base URL

- aggregators to PAMS include:
  - publisher/hosting service
  - title
  - ISSN
  - start date
  - end date
  - embargo period
  - full-text delivery format
  - base URL.
- Libraries communicate to publishers/hosting services or subscriptions agents the titles to which they wish to have access.
- Libraries communicate to PAMS information about aggregations and single titles that PAMS will manage for libraries.
- PAMS communicates to libraries holdings information about aggregations and single titles to which they subscribe.
- Publishers/hosting services and aggregators communicate to libraries prices and titles they include in their e-journal collections.

Figure 3.1 is a model of communication that illustrates the scenario when libraries use all the electronic journal services from one company. PAMS is a relatively new arrival on the library market. The concept of the company that provides stand-alone electronic services is the result of an explosive growth of online journals, aggressive aggregation, changeable access conditions and variable pricing models. PAMS fills in the service gap left by the traditional library vendors, such as Innovative Interfaces, Endeavor Information Systems,

Figure 3.1 Flowchart of serials subscriptions data exchange

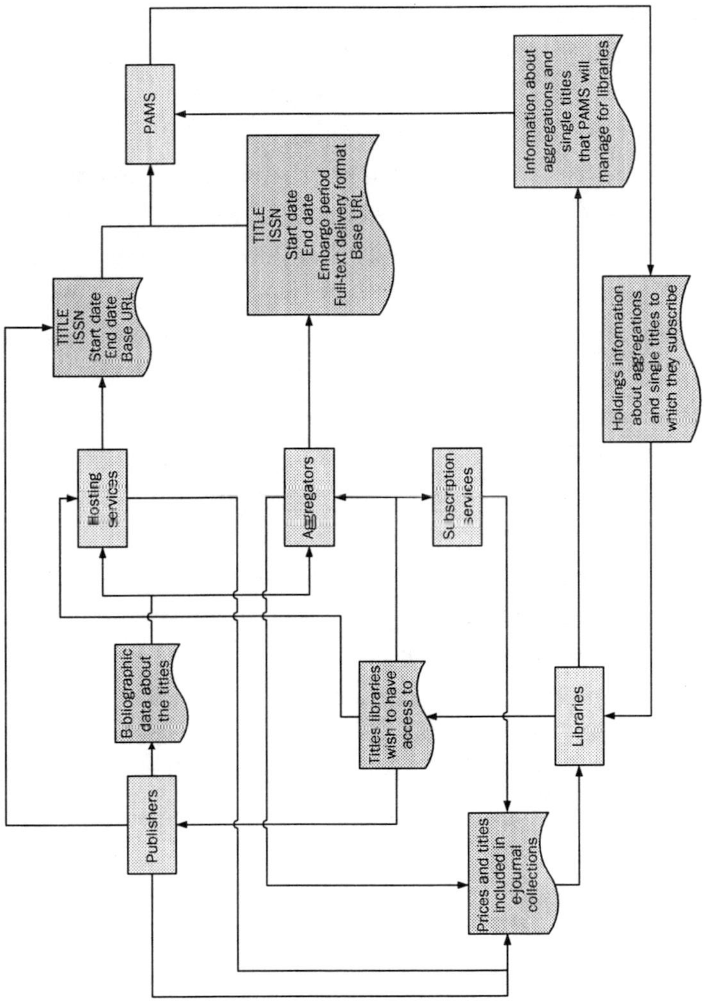

Ex Libris and others, whose main business is to provide ILS and other library technology.

Most of these companies were the first to develop new electronic technology services, such as federated searching, OpenURL link resolvers and ERM system modules. However, they are not in the business of cataloging or aggregation management of e-journals, two sorely needed services conditioning success in library management of online serials. When companies like Serials Solutions were founded their primary focus was on managing title lists of electronic journals. Very quickly, however, they realized that it was not enough and that their online repositories, databases or knowledge bases can be utilized in more ways than one. Thus they branched into territory traditionally held by library technology vendors. In direct competition to Endeavor, Ex Libris and others, they developed their own link resolvers and federated searching products, thus providing libraries with an option of using PAMS as the answer to most of their electronic technology needs. In a way, that gave libraries too much choice of which service from which company to use, and thus presented them with a dilemma over the best course of action.

Traditionally, once the library chose its ILS provider it stayed with the same vendor for other products if they were available. Obvious exceptions would be libraries in a consortium environment, where selected product procurement is decided on behalf of all participants. However, if a library has a certain degree of flexibility and wants to acquire a product from another vendor, whether because of superior quality, better pricing or unavailability of service from its current provider, it still needs to grapple with the choices available on the market.

Primary considerations inevitably relate to the problems of technological compatibility with legacy systems and pricing of the new products. Both of these issues are usually beyond the purview of the cataloging departments (including the author's own), so in the interest of this book one can consider them settled. From this point on there are several factors that weigh into the product selection decision.

- A library needs to align its short-term goals with future objectives. If the library currently is ready to implement only one type of service, e.g. an e-journal title list, it needs to look into its future plans for implementing other products, e.g. an OpenURL link resolver, and ascertain whether the vendor of choice is capable of providing this service in the future.

- A library needs to explore whether the service of current priority is available as a value-added product in combination with other purchases. For instance, if a library's ultimate goal is to buy sets of MARC records from a vendor, it may get A–Z listing as part of its subscription, rather than buying the title list service first from one company and then implementing MARC records from another.

- A library needs to consider the size of the vendor's repository, or knowledge base, and coordinate it with the desired services.

An example of the latter situation arose when California State University, Northridge implemented a MARC records service from Serials Solutions; this provided instant catalog access to almost 25,000 electronic journals. Meanwhile, the A–Z list and link resolver were Ex Libris products (MetaLib and SFX) rooted in the SFX knowledge base, which consisted of only 15,000 titles. The SFX knowledge base's title composition has been slowly catching up with the number of MARC records available from Serials Solutions. However, for a long time there was a 10,000-title discrepancy, which left reference librarians and users wondering why a journal had a record in the catalog but was not listed in the A–Z list; by the same token users would never know what journals were missed by the SFX link resolver because they were not within the scope of the SFX knowledge base.

Ex Libris technology was implemented in the library on the 23-campus consortium level, while Serials Solutions MARC records was the choice at the local level. Fortunately, the systems administrator, Eric Willis, found a creative solution to the problem of asynchronization between the A–Z journal title list and catalog-based access to the online journals. He redirected the search indexes on the page of *CSUN List of Electronic Periodicals* by programming them to run a catalog search (instead of going to the A–Z list), by *title*, *key word*, *subject* and *ISSN/e-ISSN*, all limited to electronic journals – and *voilà!* The library got an accurate listing of its electronic periodicals. Moreover, to respect users' habits and website integrity he retained the look of the page as it had appeared when the query went into the MetaLib knowledge base (Figures 3.2 and 3.3).

Libraries need to keep in mind that the functionality of electronic technology services, such as title lists, OpenURL linking and MARC record batch loading, is based on the vendor's knowledge base, and it is the size and composition of this knowledge base that will determine the capability of the library service. Having knowledge-base-based services originating from different vendors, and thus from different databases, may create mismatched levels of title availability.

In summary, when deciding which vendor or vendors to choose, libraries should be asking a number of questions.

Figure 3.2 MetaLib look-alike of CSUN OPAC e-journal search screen

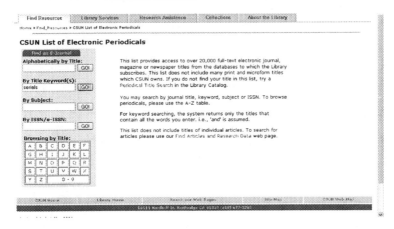

Figure 3.3 Title browse screen of e-journal search results at CSUN

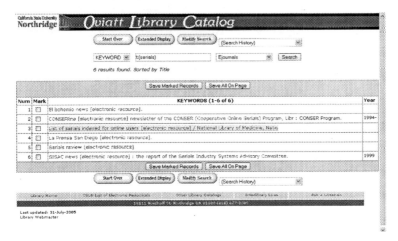

For the library:

- What are the short- and long-term goals of implementing an electronic serials management structure? List the services of first priority and create a 'wish' list.

- What is the price the library is ready to pay for the initial purchase of the service and its future maintenance?

- How well would the vendor's technology integrate with legacy systems?

- In case of services provided by more than one vendor, will the services be compatible with each other and the ILS?

- Are there staff to implement and support the service?

- Can we, ourselves, find out about other libraries' experiences working with this vendor/service?

For the vendor(s):

- What kind of electronic journals management services do you provide?

- What kind of service may be a value-added item with a purchase of another product?

- What kind of customization can you provide?

- What distinguishes you from your competitors?

- What is the cost of the initial purchase and future maintenance?

- What level of technological expertise is required from the library personnel administering the services?

- What kind of customer support do you provide?

- How long is an average implementation period?

- Do you work directly with publishers/aggregators/subscription agents, or do you use public data?

- How often do you provide updates?

- Can you provide us with references from libraries you currently work with?

As new companies emerge on the scene, old ones change hands or others branch into new services and products, libraries have to adjust to the constantly changing vendor landscape. In order to be nimble and cost-effective, libraries need to create a repository of shared experiences. Some of it appears on various e-mail listserves; those who subscribe and have time to read definitely benefit from the lively exchange and camaraderie. Some experiences are shared through articles, books and presentations. It would be helpful, however, to have a central reference service, similar to the Better Business Bureau, that would keep track of libraries' collective wisdom of working with various companies on technology and service implementations, customer service experiences, etc.

Sitko et al., in their article on e-journal management systems, encouraged libraries to exchange experiences: 'As libraries enter into relationships with new vendors offering new services, shared experiences are critical so that others may benefit by avoiding pitfalls and anticipating costs, as well as profit by gaining a deeper understanding of current e-journal management services.'[25] The challenges of e-journal management continue to grow, multiplied by the number of libraries developing e-journal collections and by the burgeoning number of electronic journals themselves, thus increasing the value of shared experiences for the entire library community.

Notes

1   Inger, Simon (2001) 'The importance of aggregators', *Learned Publishing*, 14(4): 287–90.
2   Calhoun, Karen and Kara, Bill (2000) 'Aggregation or aggravation? Optimizing access to full-text journals', *ALCTS Newsletter Online*, 11(1); available at: *http://archive.ala.org/alcts/alcts_news/v11n2/gateway_pap15.html* (accessed: 19 November 2006).

3 Martin, Charity K. and Hoffman, Paul (2002) 'Do we catalog or not? How research libraries provide bibliographic access to electronic journals in aggregated databases', *Serials Librarian*, 43(1): 61–77.

4 Jones, Ed (2002) *The Exchange of Serials Subscription Information: A White Paper Prepared for the National Information Standards Organization, with Support from the Digital Library Federation*. Bethesda, MD: NISO Press.

5 *CONSER Cataloging Manual,* Module 31, Remote Access Electronic Serials. Washington, DC: Serial Record Division, Library of Congress, updated 2004; available at: *www.loc.gov/acq/conser/Module31.pdf* (accessed: 18 February 2007).

6 Wilson, David L. (1991) 'Testing time for electronic journals', *Chronicle of Higher Education*, 38(3): A22–4.

7 *Directory of Scholarly Electronic Journal and Academic Discussion Lists, 2000*, Association of Research Libraries; available at: *http://db.arl.org/dsej/start.html* (accessed: 18 February 2007).

8 Sitko, Michelle, Tafuri, Narda, Szczyrbak, Gregory and Park, Taemin (2002) 'E-journal management systems: trends, trials, and trade-offs', *Serials Review*, 28(3): 176–94.

9 Markwith, Michael, Antonucci-Durgan, Dana Ellen, Gombo, Ugen and Loghry, Pat (2005) 'Where did that e-journal go? E-journal changes and access problems', *Serials Librarian*, 48(3/4): 243–5.

10 Jones, note 4 above.

11 Available at: *www.serialssolutions.com/aboutus/default .asp* (accessed: 20 August 2006).

12 Mays, Allison P. (2001) 'Profiles encouraged, company profile: Serials Solutions, LLC', *Against the Grain*, 13(4): 58.

13 McCracken, Peter (2003) 'Beyond title lists: incorporating e-journals into the OPAC', *Serials Librarian*, 45(3): 101–8.

14 Available at: *http://serialssolutions.com/aboutus/abouthistory.asp* (accessed: 20 August 2006).

15 Orlo Willis, personal communication, 21 August 2006.

16 Savory, Richard (2001) 'Managing electronic e-journal access: the TDNet solution', *Serials*, 14(3): 275–82.

17 Available at: *www.tdnet.com/site/page.asp?ID=457A&parent=457* (accessed: 20 August 2006).

18 Sitko et al., note 8 above.

19 Duranceau, Ellen (2002) 'E-journal package-content tracking services', *Serials Review*, 28(1): 49–53.

20 Available at: *http://tdnet.com/site/page.asp?ID=457A&parent=457* (accessed: 20 August 2006).

21 Sitko et al., note 8 above.

22 Orlo Willis, personal communication, 15 September 2006.

23 Gorman, Michael (1998) 'The five laws of library science: then and now', *School Library Journal*, 44(7): 20–3.

24 Jones, note 4 above.

25 Sitko et al., note 8 above.

4

Local approach: experience of California State University, Northridge

With the proliferation of ubiquitous technological solutions it may appear that most libraries are already 'there'. However, serials, electronic resources and cataloging listserves consistently post requests to exchange experiences of implementation. This chapter is an attempt to share the process of step-by-step implementation of the commercial MARC record service from Serials Solutions (SS) and help libraries avoid feeling blindfolded during the course of implementation and post-implementation maintenance.

Implementation of MARC record sets from a PAMS such as SS accomplishes several things at once. It provides all the advantages of cataloging for users and libraries alike without investment of staff time and the workflow issues addressed earlier.

For patrons batch loading of electronic journal records means:

- 'one-stop shop' access to the full range of library collections regardless of format;

- an ability to search for electronic journals using the full range of public catalog indexes;

- discovering related titles in varying formats.

For libraries batch cataloging represents:

- full control of the collection for collection development purposes;
- obtaining catalog records for thousands of e-journal titles at once;
- liberation from manual maintenance of title and date coverage information and URLs.

The MARC record service provided by a PAMS, just like the companies themselves, is a relatively new phenomenon. A great deal of PR goes into promotion of a new product by any company. And, before we know it, we operate on assumptions and wishful thinking. Once we delve into the process, a few surprises are in store. Libraries should anticipate that gaining centralized access to e-journal collections very quickly, implementation time excluded, will require some compromises, rethinking and workarounds. Nothing is ever perfect, but borrowing the words of Kathryn Wesley from Clemson University, quoted by Maria Collins, she 'would rather have 17,000 pretty good records vs. 5,000 really good records. You have to do what's best for the user.'[1]

California State University, Northridge (CSUN) is a medium-size academic library with a total of about 25,000 online journal titles; it uses Millennium from Innovative Interfaces as its ILS. The author's experience is augmented by the implementation of SS records at the Getty Research Library, which uses Voyager ILS from Ex Libris (formerly from Endeavor). Although the record set was substantially smaller there, only about 5,000 records, the specificity of the library focusing primarily on art history and humanities materials presented its own challenges. A flow of implementation will be presented, distinguishing between the systems where the variation in ILS made a difference in implementation. The hope is that sharing the experience of MARC record set implementation from two institutions will answer questions from libraries considering a similar service on where to start, how to proceed and what to expect from the process.

How to prepare

The best way to prepare is plan for compromises – compromises in quality of MARC records, accuracy of the data and policy decisions.

Here is how the MARC service works.

- The library activates aggregator packages to which it has access in the SS knowledge base.
- Determines its policy on key cataloging issues with respect to vendor's records.
- Fills out a MARC profile by choosing from provided options and requests customization features.
- Receives and evaluates the first test load.
- If needed, adjusts its MARC profile and requests another test load(s).
- Receives and loads into the database the first batch of MARC records.
- If applicable, starts the clean-up process.
- Receives monthly (or more frequent) updates of 'new', 'changed' and 'deleted' records.

As you can tell, before the first load takes place a library needs to review or revise some former policy decisions.

Single- versus multiple-record approach

If a library has an electronic journal collection it has already made its choice of single- versus multiple-record approach. To summarize briefly the issues addressed earlier, here is the crux of confusion on which approach to choose. AACR2 does not have an explicit rule for the choice of approach; it merely recommends describing all aspects of the item, including its content, carrier and the type of publication. CONSER leaves the choice to libraries, suggesting using a single-record approach when print and online formats are identical in contents. Separate records are recommended when the difference in contents is significant enough not to consider them equivalents.

Most libraries started off by choosing a single-record approach, and they did so for two reasons: first, patrons favor a single record; second, when the first online journals emerged it was easier to edit the existing print record than create a new one. In addition, there was no clear guidance from cataloging standards and very few separate online records were available from the OCLC and RLIN.

When an institution is considering buying record sets, for all practical purposes it would be prudent to choose the multiple-record approach. If the library has already adopted the single record, it is okay to revise the policy and have a hybrid approach, with both types of records coexisting in the catalog. There is a reverse example of the hybrid situation. If the library has adopted a separate-record approach from the start, and it catalogs government documents by using records from the GPO, it is bound to have a mixed approach in the catalog since the GPO uses a single-record approach. So you see how online publications made us adapt to the new environment and become less rigid with the concept of database consistency.

Both SS and TDNet can make MARC sets work with a single-record approach in order for a library to keep its policy. However, by opting for, or switching to, the multiple-record approach, the library will be able to avoid the pitfalls of one process associated with the single record: a library's ILS needs to have the facility and be configured to detect duplication and allow merger of the records. Duplication detection takes place when a vendor's records are matched to the existing records. The obvious match point is the OCLC number contained in both records. Once a match is found, the records need to be merged in order to transfer URL information and other fields to the existing records. But here is what can go wrong in this situation.

- Not all records have an OCLC number. A library may not even use OCLC, and from the vendor's side non-CONSER or brief machine-generated records do not have OCLC numbers. Eighty-five per cent of SS records come from the CONSER database. This seems like a big number. However, for a collection size of 20,000 journals this translates into 3,000 titles lacking CONSER record availability. In this case the match point has to be set to the title/ISSN combination, which itself is notoriously unreliable.

- Only an online record may be available from the vendor for a print title. In this case the system may not find the match at all and the merger would have to be done manually. SS does its best to match the correct form with the title, but there are not enough ready records in its knowledge base to go around, therefore the vendor adapts the available record for the needed format. Thus a match for the print record may be the online version, and vice versa, or online titles may receive an enhanced print-format record.

Now consider future record manipulation if the print format ceases, which happens quite often. The MARC record service provides updated information for online titles only; print format is the library's responsibility. Extra effort will need to be made to remove online information from the ceased format to close the record. Another issue has to do with volatility of aggregators. Keeping track of the numerous changes is the prized feature of PAMS. In the context of the single record, every time the title changes or gets dropped by the aggregator(s), the print record would need to be matched and manipulated, which always carries the risk of a mistake. Depending on the size and type of the collection, PAMS can make the single-record approach work quite well by offering a 'hosted' links option (more about this later). But why? Additional work for the library and the mistake-prone process may not justify insistence on the single-record approach.

The experience of Wayne Morris and Lynda Thomas of Glamorgan University makes a very strong case for the separate-record approach being user-friendlier than the single one. Among advantages they list is the ability to create a subcatalog of electronic journals, alerting users to the availability of the online version through GMD and having clear online records by excluding irrelevant print information.[2]

Describing the trends in e-resource cataloging practices, Chen et al. observed that the 'growing tendency of obtaining sets of resources from the vendors and using the provided cataloging records, appear to be moving libraries away from the single record approach'.[3]

Classification

The classification of library materials, a stalwart component of cataloging, may be another opportunity for a policy compromise in the context of vendor MARC record sets.

Stemming from the early days of a manageable number of electronic resources and the prevalence of the single-record approach, more likely than not a library's policy called for classifying electronic journals.

In the case of online resources, the function of the call number as a shelving device is replaced by online virtual shelf listing for the purpose of subject collocation and display of the full range of a library's materials regardless of their format. And since there is no physical placement of the items, it has become common, including LC practice, to leave the cutter number out and use only the topic-specific classification number, or in MARC terms $a.

In addition to filing within the virtual shelf, the call numbers may serve as a cataloging device for looking up or verifying subject heading and class number correlations, and established local cataloging practices. Classification numbers can be employed in collection assessments and development decisions and used for accreditation reports in academic libraries. In other words, the call number is a very useful tool, and along with subject headings is a product of intellectual analysis of the item's contents, i.e. a very expensive piece of information.

However, only 75 per cent of SS MARC records have the call number, which means that 25 per cent, or a quarter of the load, do not. If the local practice was not to assign call numbers to online journals, this will not present a problem. The issue would rather be whether or not to change the previous policy and display the call number in those 75 per cent of the records that have it.

What if local practice called for classification of online materials? If this is the case, the library has to make some choices. It may need to change cataloging practice, or even lower its standards and let some, or all, electronic journals remain unclassified. Classifying the journals from the segment of the load lacking call numbers would be an exercise in futility, since the records may be overlayered during the next update should there be a change in aggregation or a better record becomes available. Therefore, the classification dilemma would instead center on the question of whether or not to display the call number in the records that have it.

In the case of the Getty Research Library, the author's former place of employment, the established policy was to classify electronic journals and display their call numbers. While preparing for the SS MARC records, the policy was revised and the decision made not to display the available call numbers, but still load them as part of the MARC data and keep them in the records for in-house reference cataloging needs. The local call number field (MARC tag 090) was repurposed and populated with the genre-like term 'E-journal' (the wording could differ) to be displayed in OPAC and used as a collocation device for all e-journal titles available in the library.

CSUN's pre-existing policy also called for classifying electronic journals. However, as oppose to the Getty Research Institute, the call number was used for strictly internal purposes and was never displayed in OPAC. The decision was made to accept that 25 per cent of the records would not have the call number, continue with the current policy of not displaying the available call number and not use the option of assigning a local genre-like call number field to the loaded records in order to generate a form-based collocation device.

The factors taken into account in the decisions of both libraries included established local cataloging policy; the perceived needs of the library users – scholars and researchers at the Getty, and students and faculty at CSUN; functionalities of the different ILS (Voyager and

Millennium); and display of the public interface for both systems.

There was an additional conundrum for the implementation task force at CSUN pertaining to usage of the call number. CSUN, as an academic library, has to produce accreditation reports regularly. The reports are structured according to the titles fitting within the local codes assigned to each discipline, called PDCs (program discipline codes). In her reports the collection development coordinator ties the discipline codes to the range of call numbers that fall into each discipline.

In the old days of manually cataloged records, cataloging assistants assigned the PDCs to each record by hand. In the automated cataloging environment, however, the library was about to lose the PDC assignment, which was unacceptable to the collections development coordinator. Like most libraries, CSUN previously could afford to catalog only a small portion of its electronic journal collection: out of a total of 25,000 journals no more than 5,000 were cataloged. However, each of those 5,000 records had a PDC code embedded in it. Now all these records were about to be replaced by the SS records. Some local fields, including the field carrying the PDC information (940), could be protected from the overlay; and a goal of the task group formed to implement the SS MARC service was not only to keep valuable local information intact but also to find a way to utilize the available call numbers to the maximum, especially for collection development purposes. The solution again came from the systems administrator. He devised a way of automatically assigning PDC codes to the records during the load by mapping the call numbers in the SS records to the table of PDC codes. The result was beautiful – all 75 per cent of the records with call numbers received their PDCs during the loading process.

Direct versus hosted links

SS offers two ways to display holdings information in the record: through direct and 'hosted' links. Assuming that a library uses 856 for its URL information, direct linking means that the number of links in the OPAC record will be equal to the number of databases, aggregations and hosting services from which the journal is available. The displayed link will have information on the name of the access provider and coverage dates, and if the $z (public note) is used will have an embedded URL to the source (if the library does not use $z the full syntax of the URL may appear). The user will be taken directly from the record to the title screen of the journal in the corresponding database (Figure 4.1).

There are two advantages to this method from the user's standpoint. One is that no extra steps or clicks are required when connecting to the journals. The other, equally

Figure 4.1   **CSUN example of direct links**

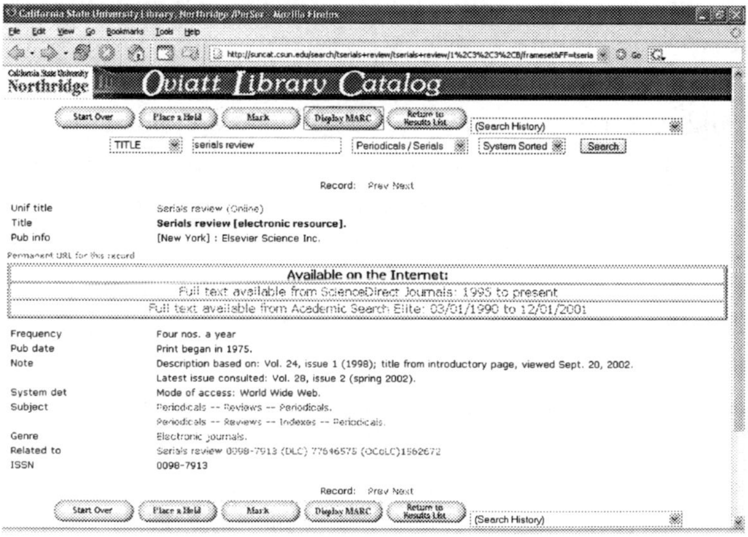

136

important, is that the patron is not only able to see directly from the OPAC record how many and which databases provide access to the title, but can see the coverage dates in the context of the bibliographic record and choose the preferred source of access. Not all interfaces are created equal, and some are more user-friendly and functional than others. Librarians and users alike have preferences developed in accordance with their information-seeking needs and favored delivery options. The holdings data provided via direct links reside in the library catalog and the URLs have library proxy server strings embedded in them:

> http://libproxy.csun.edu:2048/login?url=http://www
> .sciencedirect.com/science/journal/00987913lzFull text
> available from ScienceDirect Journals: 1995 to present.

Since provider and holdings information are located on the library server, the updates of this information take place once a month with the next scheduled load. Strictly speaking, the data are current for only one day a month. However, despite the notoriety of ever-changing aggregations and access terms there is still a good chance that in the space of one month there will not be enough changes in the full volume of records to render the information useless. Still, for libraries, where having 100 per cent of holdings information up to date is vital for users, this option may not be workable.

The hosted links option means exactly that – links are hosted on the SS server. In this scenario the record contains only one generic link with customizable wording, for example 'Click for full text' (Figure 4.2). The link takes the user to another screen, which lists all access options for the title (Figure 4.3).

The obvious inconvenience is the extra link and screen that the user has to go through before accessing full text.

Figure 4.2 San Diego State University example of hosted links

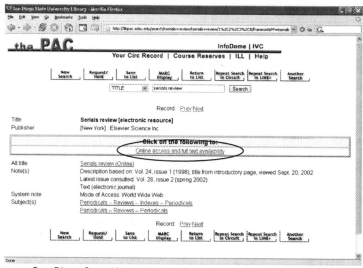

Source: San Diego State University Library online catalog

Figure 4.3 Hosted links reside on SS server

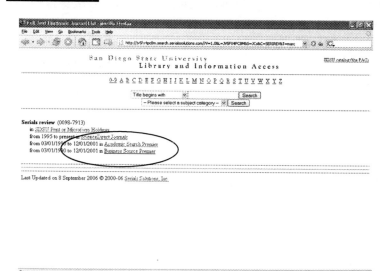

Many users may find this confusing and unnecessary, since their goal is to get to the full text as soon as possible. Using this option will most likely require additionally educating users on the process of accessing full text. The advantage of this option consists in daily updates of the holdings data. This is possible because holdings data reside on the SS server. By clicking the URL in the title record, the user in fact sends a search query to the library's SS portal to find corresponding providers and coverage dates:

http://JV5FX4PC8M.search.serialssolutions.com/?
V=1.0&L=JV5FX4PC8M&S=JCs&C=SERIREV&T=
marc.

It is important to note that the record's URL in this option connects to the SS server. This means that all information about content providers and coverage dates is stored with SS. It may also mean that access to the resources depends on the availability of the SS portal. Any problems with the SS site, other than scheduled maintenance, which does not affect hosting services, may cut off a library's access to all its electronic journals in the database. Without trying to paint a gloomy 'what if?' scenario, this consideration may be vital for libraries that prefer to have control over data rather than relinquish it to another party. Comparing direct versus hosted links in this respect prompts a fair analogy of dating PAMS versus getting married to it – with all the pluses and minuses that go with each decision (Table 4.1).

Since aggregators' links are stored off site and are not part of the bibliographic record, any changes (typically to the providers' URL and coverage data) will be caught promptly and will not affect a library's access to the journals. Thus the monthly load of 'change' records from SS requires much less work, reflecting changes occurring only to bibliographic

| Table 4.1 | Comparison of direct and hosted links from SS |

Option	Advantages	Disadvantages
Direct links	One-click access to the full text Links in the context of bibliographic information Choice of provider from bibliographic record URL and coverage data stored in OPAC	Data updated only once a month No title usage statistics Increased number of 'change' records during monthly updates
Hosted links	Daily data updates Title usage statistics Reduced number of 'change' records during monthly updates	Extra click/screen to access full text Provider and coverage data stored in SS portal Access to journals depends on functionality of SS portal

information itself and not to URLs. In addition, the hosted link option can provide title usage statistics since every search is registered in the SS client center.

CSUN opted to have direct links. The main reason for this choice was the extra screen to get to the full text, which was felt would confuse students. It was thought that having data updated only once a month would not present a problem for users. But, after having the MARC service implemented for almost a year, there have been quite a few situations when an aggregator drops a title and CSUN records would still show for another few weeks that the library had it, which combined with other misleading coverage data (more about this later) makes the service and the catalog information look unreliable. It is another example of gaining something and losing something. By providing instant access to almost 25,000 electronic journals, CSUN did lose some control over the accuracy of the data in the catalog. It is quite likely that the decision on hosted versus direct links at CSUN will be reviewed sometime in the future. Fortunately for the libraries that decide to change linking options, SS has an easy process to do so. For hosted links the service is available immediately or with the next update; switching from hosted to direct links would take place with the next update.

Title composition

Depending on the profile of the library, there are two aspects of MARC service title selection that need to be addressed during the implementation process. The first is germane to libraries that have scope-specific collections, such as the humanities or science. The subject coverage within an aggregation may vary significantly enough to span several disciplines, with some of them falling outside the primary focus of the library's collection. Providing access through A–Z lists, using such aggregations as Lexis-Nexis as a news and transcripts database, is one thing, but cataloging journals accessible through that database is another. This issue came up during an SS implementation process at the Getty Research Library, which focuses primarily on art history and humanities materials.

During the time of manual cataloging, in order to remain within the research subject of the collection, only journals from relevant aggregations and relevant journals from generalized aggregations, like Lexis-Nexis, were added to the catalog. The MARC record service, with several clicks in the client center, enables all journals from all aggregations to be added to the collection.

The question arose as to whether the library indeed wanted all those journals integrated into the catalog, which would substantially dilute the art history/humanities concentration and introduce new and irrelevant subject headings. Adding social science journals was fine, but populating the catalog with banking and law publications was a dubious enterprise. The decision was passed to the top management echelon of the Getty Research Institute, and the verdict came down to take full advantage of the MARC service and include all available titles in the library's catalog.

The second aspect of the MARC service title composition pertains equally to specialized and comprehensive collections. The issue is about including free open-access journals and government documents in the catalog. The SS knowledge base contains 30 free journal databases, including Directory of Open Access Journals, Public Library of Science (PLoS), U.S. Government Documents, Making of America Journals (Cornell) and many others. For specialized libraries the relevance and target audience of those journals may serve as the criteria for selection, but it may not be the case for all-inclusive collections. In cases like these the decision may be purely financial.

The SS pricing model is based upon the number of MARC records supplied to the library. If adding free journals would increase the number of records and bump the price up to the next bracket, making the service unaffordable altogether, then obviously the decision would be against such inclusion. If, however, the library could afford the next pricing tier, it becomes necessary to evaluate if enhancing the collection with free peer-reviewed journals is worth the extra fiscal outlay. In case of CSUN, which has a comprehensive collection supporting the university's undergraduate curriculum, the dean of the library gave the implementation group a green light to add as many open-access and government publications as was deemed appropriate; the government documents database was added after consultation with the govdocs librarian.

Getting started

Once a library decides on the principal access and classification issues, it needs to create an e-journal portal in its SS client center. In other words, it needs to notify the service of all the databases to which the library has access. The SS knowledge base contains 1,317 databases and 107,800 unique titles, and about 175 are added every week.[4] The subscription to the MARC service includes the Access and Management Suite (AMS), with such features as A–Z listing and overlap analysis. So if the library does not have a similar service from another vendor it will get it as part of the SS MARC package. This would be an example of a clear benefit of having A–Z list and MARC record services originating from the same knowledge base. Creating the e-journal title profile takes place in the data management area of the SS portal. Surprisingly, to date there is no browsing capability to see a list of all available aggregations and databases. If you want to do that, you have to hoax the system by doing a search on each letter of the alphabet, for example databases starting with 'a' (Figure 4.4). The trick is to know your ABCs and search on every letter and even a number (Figure 4.5).

It is surprising for the portal of such a sophisticated service not to have a pretty basic browse function or an option for 'all' in its e-catalog search. After all, it is only 1,230 databases and seeing all of them, not just searching under individual names, could be quite an educational experience for many librarians. Right now one has to know the name of the database exactly as it is established by SS to find it in the knowledge base. Hopefully, this enhancement will take place some time in the near future. It is easier to see the list of providers, as they appear in the drop-down menu under the provider name search.

Figure 4.4 SS workaround database browse screen of databases starting with a letter

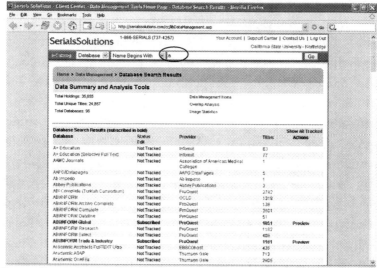

Source: Screenshot from SS CSUN portal

Figure 4.5 SS workaround database browse screen of databases starting with a number

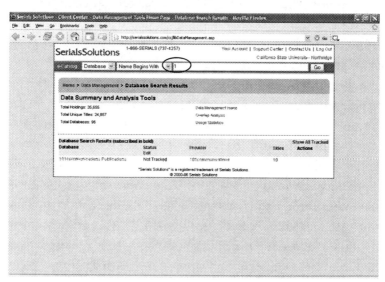

Source: Screenshot from SS CSUN portal

With the list of its databases and/or content providers in hand, the library needs to find and activate them in the data management section. This process consists of searching the name of the database and changing the status from 'not tracked' to 'tracked'.

The activation of titles in the database can be handled on the database level or at the title-by-title level. Database-level activation works when the library has subscriptions to 100 per cent of the titles in the database. Having title-level activation is important when libraries subscribe to only part of the contents of the aggregator. Partial contents, however, may still comprise hundreds of titles, and it would be very time-consuming to activate the titles in the partial databases one by one. SS, known for its customer service, has a solution for a hurdle like that: a library e-mails spreadsheets of the titles that need to be activated, SS uploads the data into the library's journal portal and titles get activated automatically.

This was a very helpful and time-saving solution for CSUN, which is part of the California State University consortium and receives a lot of subscription data from the chancellor's office in the form of Excel spreadsheets. The spreadsheets contain information on titles, ISSNs and coverage dates as applied to all the libraries in the consortium. Spreadsheets of titles comprising only partial database coverage were e-mailed to SS for uploading. The company's policy is to upload spreadsheets that contain more than 100 titles, but it was nice enough to do it for CSUN for smaller databases as well.

A word of caution here. As CSUN discovered during the evaluation of the first test MARC records, the coverage dates from the Excel spreadsheets *do not* get uploaded to the journal portal. Instead, the coverage in the SS portal is set for the generic database default. When CSUN started SS implementation, its understanding was that the company customizes coverage data to the library level, meaning that the access dates information will be specific to each library; that turned out not to be the case. This is probably the biggest misconception libraries have about SS MARC record services. The dates associated with a title or entire database in the e-journal portal mean coverage available in general for a certain title from a certain aggregator, not the coverage for your particular library for your patrons.

In Figure 4.6 the databases in bold in this screenshot of the *Serials Review* record are the ones to which CSUN has a subscription. The dates in bold that correspond to the databases represent the coverage dates available in general, not the dates available for *your library*. SS does no date customization for libraries. If a library's coverage differs from the generally available dates, supplied by the publisher,

Figure 4.6 Example of *Serials Review* journal available from different databases

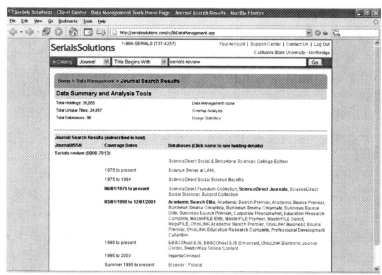

Source: Screenshot from SS CSUN portal

the library needs to customize dates in the portal manually, whether on a database or a title level. Customized dates will take precedence over the default ones, and the holdings information in the note will be downloaded accurately to reflect local journal access.

Meeting the challenges

In preparation for the MARC records download ScienceDirect was by far the most challenging database to work on. Not only did CSUN have access to just part of the titles, through a consortium agreement, but those titles had coverage dates that did not match the default database dates and were not in concert with each other either. It seemed like having accurate date ranges required a lot of manual intervention, which the library was trying to avoid. The problem was solved by setting the uniform customized coverage dates applicable to most of the titles first, and then customizing the remainder. Fortunately, the SS portal allows for such manipulation. In summary, here are the steps CSUN took to activate ScienceDirect titles and establish customized coverage.

1. Verify the list of titles to which your library has access through ScienceDirect (Figure 4.7).

2. Send SS a spreadsheet of the titles to be uploaded to the portal (Figure 4.7).

3. If your coverage dates differ from the database's default dates, follow the path:
   Home>Data Management>Elsevier>ScienceDirect Journals.

4. Click on 'Edit' (Figure 4.8) to customize the dates at the library level and set the date range available for the majority of the library's ScienceDirect titles (Figure 4.9), and save changes.

Figure 4.7 ScienceDirect, verification and upload of titles to SS e-journal portal

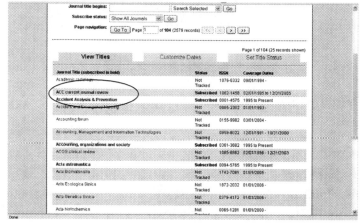

Source: Screenshot from SS CSUN ScienceDirect portal

Figure 4.8 ScienceDirect, step 1 in customization of dates in SS e-journal portal

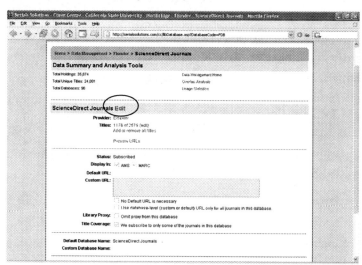

Source: Screenshot from SS CSUN ScienceDirect portal

5. At this point your dates are set for all titles available to your library through ScienceDirect subscription. If your ScienceDirect titles have uniform coverage, stop here.

Figure 4.9 ScienceDirect, step 2 in customization of dates in SS e-journal portal

Source: Screenshot from SS CSUN ScienceDirect portal

6. If you have variations on an individual title level, then once you save the changes to the database-level date's customization click on the link displaying the number of available titles (Figure 4.10). This takes you to the screen listing of ScienceDirect titles.

7. Search for 'Selected titles' and you will arrive at ScienceDirect titles available to your library and set to your customized date range (Figure 4.11).

8. Click on the 'Customize dates' tab to edit coverage range for the titles that deviate from the dates available for most titles (Figure 4.12).

Although it is time-consuming, it is not an impossible task to complete, and most other aggregations do not require such scrupulous navigation. A note to keep in mind: since partial-coverage databases like ScienceDirect and similar are activated on the basis of information from the library, not

Figure 4.10 ScienceDirect, step 3 in customization of dates in SS e-journal portal

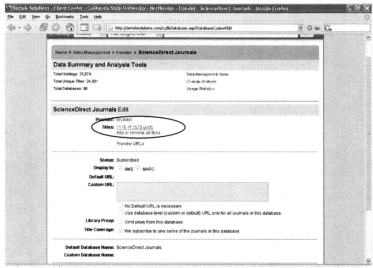

Source: Screenshot from SS CSUN ScienceDirect portal

Figure 4.11 ScienceDirect, step 4 in customization of dates in SS e-journal portal

Source: Screenshot from SS CSUN ScienceDirect portal

Figure 4.12 ScienceDirect, step 5 in customization of dates in SS e-journal portal

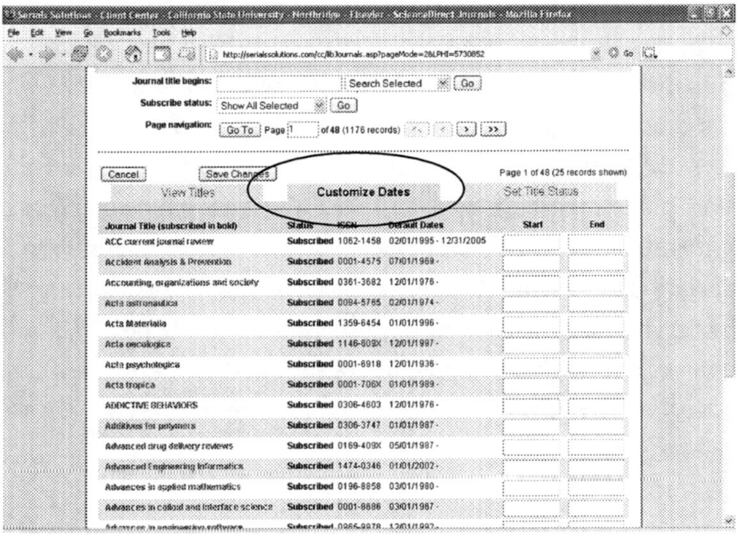

Source: Screenshot from SS CSUN ScienceDirect portal

the publisher, it is the library's responsibility to add or take away titles from its custom packages in accordance with its subscription terms. SS maintains titles in aggregations that comprise the entire Elsevier package, not the local variants; if Elsevier discontinues publication of a journal, SS drops it from the aggregation. If, however, it is the library's subscription composition that has changed and a title was unsubscribed by the library but still generally remains available, the library needs to go in the portal and 'deactivate' the title itself.

Single journals

SS is known for managing aggregations, and the question may be asked 'What about the single journals, i.e. journals subscribed directly from the publisher?' Even though single journals do not present the same maintenance problems as aggregations, they still need to be cataloged and their coverage dates kept up to date.

To satisfy this need SS created a database with an appropriate name, 'Single journals', with content providers stated as 'multiple vendors'. Currently there are over 1,200 titles collocated in this database. The activation of journals takes place on a title-by-title basis. As with partial-coverage aggregations, it is the library's responsibility to 'deactivate' a journal from the database should the subscription be discontinued. If a journal's publication has ceased, SS will remove it from the single journals database and send the record to the library with the next update as part of the 'deletes' file.

MARC profile

Once the library activates the journal packages and single journals for which it wishes to receive MARC records, the next step is filling in the MARC profile form, which SS will use to customize the library's records.

The level of customization by SS is very high and, according to the author's communications with the company during the process, there is no MARC field that it cannot customize, add or delete on a library's request. Filling out the MARC profile is a good place for the library to review and/or revise its current policies, since the number of loaded records will be substantial enough to affect the look and feel of the library's journal collection reflected in the catalog.

The issues that should be reviewed run from single versus separate records, aggregator-neutral records, restriction notes and general cataloging standards of the journal records. Regarding the latter, as one goes along the implementation process it becomes clear that expectations of perfect cataloging have no place in a vendor-supplied records system. This is not to say that SS does not do its best in providing quality records – it does.

A paradigm shift in priorities is taking place in technical services across the country and around the world. The LC recently adopted access-level records for monographs and announced[5] adoption of access-level records for serials, affirming that in current conditions it is far more important to provide *access* to resources than to belabor perfect cataloging quality. And frankly, that is what users want. All too often catalogers forget the real users whom we ultimately serve, getting carried away by issues important to catalogers only. We take our knowledge and understanding of MARC records for granted and expect readers to appreciate everything we have done for them. And sometimes they do not. This is not to advocate the lowest common denominator; instead it should reassure catalogers that their job of exposing more of a library's resources to users is far more valued by patrons than having fewer resources expressed through perfect records.

At CSUN, with its 33,000 students, librarians have faculty status and are expected to perform a wide variety of tasks. Serving on the reference desk, whether one is a technical services librarian or a public service one, is mandatory. It was a quite uncomfortable but very eye-opening experience for the author in the beginning to get out of the cataloging closet and go public. It gave a whole new appreciation of what one does as a cataloger, both in a good and in a bad sense. One learned that as long as the students and faculty find what they want in the catalog, they do not really care how it looks or know how it *should* look, nor can they make sense of the record's elements. Dates in the 1xx, 6xx and 7xx fields would be taken for the publication date, and subject headings could as well be titles. Once the search retrieved the record, all they want to know is where in the library the book is located and where to click to gain online access (clicking on the hyperlinked phrase 'Click for online access' does not always seem to be self-explanatory).

CSUN has a very extensive information literacy program, which in 2005 enabled 22,000 students to attend bibliographic instruction lectures at the library; nevertheless there seem to be an endless stream of users who do not know what to make of the record once they find it – and those are the ones who are bold enough to ask for an explanation at the reference desk. There is no count of the students who give up without ever asking for help. Other universities may have different experiences with their users, but CSUN is one of 23 campuses in the California State University system – the largest educational system in the country – so what does it say about our real user, not the imaginary, wished-for one? Development of the new cataloging rules entitled Resource Description and Access (RDA) is an encouraging move towards real users and real priorities. Emphasizing *access* over description not only goes along with FRBR concepts but also fulfills the requirements and expectations of today's user to be able to find as much information as possible online and access it effortlessly.

The mere fact that vendor record sets are becoming a reality for so many libraries is a tribute to the reprioritizing movement in the cataloging process. RDA in fact will be a much-needed theoretical support to what is happening in practice. And while RDA rules are being written, libraries can continue inching forward towards access as a priority by working with vendors in populating their catalogs with records that will be hard at work providing access: first by their sheer numbers, and second by focusing on access to the resources and not their description.

This will become clear once we examine what to expect when loading SS MARC records.

SS provides a MARC record template for the library to complete. The form is downloaded from the SS client center, saved locally, filled out and sent back to SS as an attachment; the vendor then uses the profile to customize records for the library. The profile can be modified at any time at no charge, whether as a result of the test record evaluation process or after the go-live production phase.

This section describes the SS MARC record profile filled out by CSUN, with some explanations. The options in this example pertain to cataloging decisions only; no systems preferences are discussed.

Update method options

The choice here is between modifying the existing body of records or loading new ones every update. To modify the existing records the library receives three types of files: new, changes and deletes.

New records

Records can be new for several reasons.

- A new title has been added to the SS knowledge base and is part of an aggregation to which the library subscribes.

- A title moved from an aggregator outside the library's profile to an aggregator to which the library has a subscription.

- As CSUN found out during the first months of implementation, the title can be erroneously deactivated in the library portal by SS. It may be sent as a 'delete' title one month, then reactivated without any intervention from the library and sent the following month as a 'new' title.

It was a mystery to CSUN why this last problem happens, but the library learned to deal with it. When the 'deletes' file is received, titles are not deleted automatically: the library goes through every one of them (usually under 50 per load) and verifies if indeed library/aggregator has lost access to the title. Once CSUN confirms that the access is lost, the record is deleted. Very often, however, the library still has perfectly good access to the title, and in this case it does nothing except keep the record printout in a special folder until the next update. Since CSUN chose direct links, updates take place only once a month. Many things can happen in a month that SS is aware of and yet CSUN is not, so this folder is a sort of quarantine for the 'delete' records under watch. Frequently, if a record is not deleted, the next update brings it as part of the 'new' file.

SS could not give a definitive answer as to why this is happening, but said it was working hard to improve its algorithms. In CSUN's experience the improvement did take place, because the number of records incorrectly marked for deletion became substantially smaller over time in comparison with the first few loads.

Change records

The question is, what constitutes change for SS? A changed record is defined as one where any or all of the bibliographic contents, coverage dates or URL syntax have changed since the last update received by the library. For example, the month after EBSCO switched from search.epnet.com to search.ebscohost.com, CSUN received a 'change' file that equaled its EBSCO holdings.

Delete records

Similar to new records, records are included in the 'delete' file for several reasons.

- The title ceased publication and was deleted from the SS knowledge base.
- The title moved from an aggregation to which a library has access to one where the library has no access.
- The title gets erroneously 'deactivated' from the library's profile by a bug in the program. This happens quite often and is a reason why libraries should be careful about deleting records automatically.

Replacing all records

SS also offers an option of delivering a completely new set of records each time. The convenience of this is that there is no need to manage 'change' and 'delete' files because records from the previous load get deleted and the new ones loaded as replacement.

On the other hand, there are more issues to consider than just the frightening thought of deleting and replacing thousands of records every month. First and foremost, CSUN has quite a few order records that were transferred from the existing record to the SS record during post-load clean-up. This makes the loading of a new file every time, and the deletion of all existing records, impossible. In addition, using its local Innovative ILS, CSUN was able to protect certain local fields from the overlay – for example, acquisition and local bibliographic notes. This is its way of adding customized information to a title in a vendor-record environment. By opting to delete existing records and load a new set with every update, we would lose the ability to retain valuable local information in selected records.

Standard edits

Table 4.2 shows the fields that will be changed in every record. These changes reflect SS as the source of the records.

Record selection

The decision on the record selection is a very important one. A library's preferences will define the body of the entire e-journal collection, as every choice will translate into hundreds, if not thousands, of records. It is also one of the places where the imperfection, as well as convenience, of vendor records will show the most. Libraries need to be aware that there are not enough perfectly matched records for every online title. Most records in the SS knowledge base were not created for the online format of materials but were made 'online' by addition of some format-specific elements, such as the uniform title with (Online) qualifier. Combining the physical description area (field 300) that details the

Table 4.2   Standard edits in SS records

Field	Description
LDR_05	Will be either 'n', 'c' or 'd', based on the record's status as *new*, *corrected* or *deleted* at your institution
001	Insert an SS-generated journal-specific control number
003	This will read 'WaSeSS', the SS MARC organization code
005	Insert date and time of last SS modification
035	Delete original; replace with content of 001, preceded by 'WaSeSS'
040	Append '|dWaSeSS' to existing list of organization codes

number of volumes and physical size of the publication with 130s (Online) and 245 $h [electronic resource] makes records look like cataloging oxymorons. However, all these records carry well-managed URLs and coverage dates, and that is what is important for the user.

CSUN's preferences for record types offered by SS are as follows.

- *CONSER online records*. The records from the CONSER database created specifically for the online format.

- *CONSER 'neutral' records*. The format-neutral records from the CONSER database, created for an unspecified format. These records serve as the basis for creation of online-specific records.

- *CONSER print*. The records from the CONSER database created for print format but transformed into online format by addition of format-specific fields and qualifiers.

- *CONSER microform records*. Similarly to the print records, these are modified from microform format to online format.

- *CONSER CD-ROM records*.

- *SS original records*. The online and format-neutral MARC 21 records created by and for SS. SS boasts an affiliation with CONSER through editing rights to CONSER records – unique for an e-resource vendor and a validation of the SS cataloging standards.

- *Vendor-generated brief records*. The format-neutral records created using MARC records from Gale and EBSCO.

- *Ulrich's brief records*. The format-neutral records generated from Ulrich's data.

- *SS supplemental brief records*.

In customizing the MARC form, SS uses as the default for the choice of record type the term 'do not use', which prompts you to look for a strong rationale to justify countering the default. When first defining the record priorities, CSUN opted out of SS supplemental brief records, assuming that the first eight types of records would be sufficient to give full title coverage. The reluctance to accept these brief records was based on their quality and on the fact that they have to be deleted and reloaded every update.

In terms of cataloging these records represent machine-generated 'three-line wonders', containing only uniform title, main title entry, customized add-ons and URLs (Figure 4.13). Because it was very hard trying to maintain acceptable cataloging standards it was decided that these records did not meet them, and their anticipated small quantity would not affect CSUN's MARC record service.

This initial decision contained fallacies revealed only after the first production load. The gap between the number of titles marked for initial download, i.e. 20,000, and the number of records actually loaded was more than 5,000 records. This disparity made CSUN quickly reverse the

Figure 4.13 Example of SS brief record

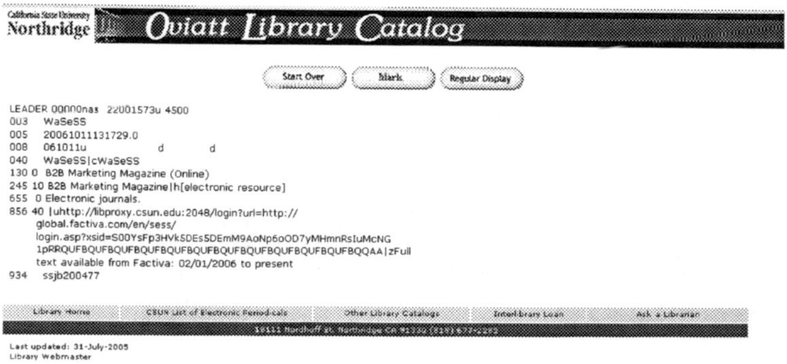
California State University Northridge
Oviatt Library Catalog

Start Over | Mark | Regular Display

LEADER 00000nas 22001573u 4500
003 WaSeSS
005 20061011131729.0
008 061011u d d
040 WaSeSS|cWaSeSS
130 0 B2B Marketing Magazine (Online)
245 10 B2B Marketing Magazine|h[electronic resource]
655 0 Electronic journals.
856 40 |uhttp://libproxy.csun.edu:2048/login?url=http://global.factiva.com/en/sess/login.asp?xsid=S00YsFp3HVk5DEs5DEmM9AoNp6oOD7yMHmnRsIuMcNG1pRRQUFBQUFBQUFBQUFBQUFBQUFBQUFBQUFBQUFBQUFBQQAA|zFull text available from Factiva: 02/01/2006 to present
934 ssjb200477

Library Home | CSUN List of Electronic Periodicals | Other Library Catalogs | Interlibrary Loan | Ask a Librarian

Last updated: 31-July-2005
Library Webmaster

Source: CSUN online catalog

supplemental record decision and thus achieve 100 per cent record coverage. The user was a winner in this reversal, since 5,000 more records were added to the database, providing online access to the corresponding number of journals.

In addition to the very basic set of MARC fields, the supplemental records do not have assigned permanent SS title ID and hence cannot be used for matching purposes during the load. Thus the entire set of brief records has to be deleted with every update and new records need to be loaded. SS is currently working on an enhancement that would enable assignment of stable brief record identifiers and so eliminate the need to delete these records with every load.

Customization options

SS has a capacity for extensive MARC field customization. If you do not like certain cataloging conventions and always wished you had one certain field present in every record, this is your chance to make it a reality without much effort or manual intervention. In its MARC profile template SS offers some default choices based on their popularity with libraries. CSUN has retained certain default choices and changed others to comply with local cataloging practices and rationale (explained in Table 4.3).

Table 4.3   Customization of SS MARC profile

Field	Possible action	Requested action	Explanation
LDR_06	Change from 'a' for 'Language material' to 'm' for 'Computer file'	Make all LDR_06 'a'	Changing LDR_06 to 'a' complies with CONSER recommendation

Table 4.3 Customization of SS MARC profile (*Cont'd*)

Field	Possible action	Requested action	Explanation
001	*Innovative clients*: Add 'OCM1' before unique identifier*	☐ Yes ☒ No	Field for SS journal ID number (ssj) that will be a match point for all subsequent loads; because of local specifics CSUN uses this field for local record number; the systems administrator configured loading tables for ssj to go into local field 934; the line from Innovative loading tables that does it is: 001|934|%> a|0|0|b|j|0|y|N|0|
006	Create or replace 006 with coding 'm\\\\\\\\\\ d\\\\\\\\\\\\'	☒ Yes ☐ No	Additional material characteristics field; coding the first byte with 'm' designates it as a record for electronic resource; overwriting existing coding in print and microfilm records will convert it from print/microfilm to online format at additional material characteristics field level; complies with CONSER
007	Create or replace 007 with coding 'cr\\n\\\\\\\\\\\\'	☒ Yes ☐ No	Physical description fixed field; similar to 006, coding as electronic resource 'c', 'r', 'n' will convert original base record to online format
008/22	Change to 's' for electronic	☒ Yes ☐ No	Form of original item 'continuing resources'; according to CONSER, online counterpart of print journal is considered original, so should be coded 's' for electronic

Table 4.3 Customization of SS MARC profile (*Cont'd*)

Field	Possible action	Requested action	Explanation
008/23	Change to 's' for electronic	☒ Yes ☐ No	Form of item 'continuing resources'; complies with CONSER practice
010 (LCCN)	Delete if present	☐ Yes ☒ No	
022 (ISSN)	Remove original and add custom 022 to all records based on title authority system, with e-ISSN in subfield a and print ISSN in subfield y	☐ Yes ☒ No	
042 (Authentication code)	Delete if present	☐ Yes ☒ No	
050 (LC call number)	Delete 050s with 'pseudo call numbers' (i.e. 'NOT IN LC', 'Microfilm', 'Discard', etc.)	☒ Yes ☐ No	This action deletes non-LC non-classification information
130 (Main entry – uniform title) *Edits to 130 and 240 are linked; select yes for both or neither*	If 130 exists, add '(Online)'; if no 130 or other 1xx exists, 130 will be constructed from 245 and appended with '(Online)'	☒ Yes ☐ No *If yes, ensure OPAC will not display both 130 and 245 fields*	CSUN's OPAC does index 130/240 for purposes other than electronic journals; nevertheless it opted to add 130/240 to every SS record for their usage in $a in the linking fields

Table 4.3   Customization of SS MARC profile (*Cont'd*)

Field	Possible action	Requested action	Explanation
222 (Key title)	Remove original and add custom 222 (or other field) to all records based on our authority title *Helpful for Innovative clients who use 222 (or other field) for their journal title index*	☐ Yes ☒ No Enter other field number here; 222 is the default	
240 (Uniform title) *Edits to 130 and 240 are linked; select yes for both or neither*	If 240 exists, add '(Online)'; if there is 110 but no 240, 240 will be constructed from 245 and appended with '(Online)'	☒ Yes ☐ No *If yes, ensure OPAC will not display both 240 and 245 fields*	See 130
245 (Title statement)	Add '|h[electronic resource]' (or other phrase) after title proper	☒ Yes ☐ No	Adding $h [electronic resource] complies with standard cataloging practice and vocabulary
300 (Physical description)	Delete if present	☒ Yes ☐ No	Complies with standard cataloging practice for electronic journals
440 (Series statement)	Add authorized name for each aggregator or publisher	☐ Yes ☒ No	Adding 440 for an aggregator would go against aggregator-neutral record policy, which CSUN has adopted

Table 4.3 Customization of **SS MARC** profile (*Cont'd*)

Field	Possible action	Requested action	Explanation
506 (Restrictions on access note)	Add phrase indicating limitations of resources (please define the phrase at right)	☐ Yes ☒ No Available only to authorized users	CSUN uses 856 $z to indicate access restrictions; adding 506 would unnecessarily clutter the record and/or violate aggregator-neutral record policy
510 (Citation/ reference notes)	Delete if present	☒ Yes ☐ No	CONSER is in the process of removing this field from the records
516 (Type of computer file or data note)	Add '|aText (electronic journal)'	☐ Yes ☒ No	According to CONSER aggregator-neutral record policy do not use this field
530 (Additional physical form)	Delete if present	☒ Yes ☐ No	Having this note for every journal with available print version may mislead the user into thinking the print form is available in the library
530 (Additional physical form)	Add '|aAlso available in print'	☐ Yes ☒ No	
533 (Reproduction note)	Delete if present	☒ Yes ☐ No	
538 (System details note)	Add 'Mode of access: World Wide Web'	☐ Yes ☒ No	CSUN users should be able to infer from other fields in the record that the journal is available via WWW; avoided cluttering the record

Table 4.3 Customization of SS MARC profile (*Cont'd*)

Field	Possible action	Requested action	Explanation
655 _0 (Genre/ form)	Add 'Electronic journals' or other phrase	☒ Yes ☐ No	Complies with local practice to add genre/ form for electronic resources
710 2_ (Added entry – corporate name)	Add authorized name for each database or publisher	☐ Yes ☒ No	Adding this field would go against aggregator-neutral record policy
856 40 (Electronic location and access)	Delete existing 856s; replace with library-specific URLs that include holdings dates and journal-specific links	Please select 856 option below	CSUN chose an option that complies with formatting other 856 fields in its catalog and lists URL, name of aggregator and coverage dates: |u[URL]|z Full text available from [database name]: [start date] to [end date]
949 (Local holdings information)	Add library-specific holdings notes information, as appropriate for your system	Enter text of field here (please label subfields)	CSUN opted out of this field for SS records

Note: *Those using an Innovative ILS are encouraged to add 'OCM1' before the SS unique identifier. This allows you to use the standard Innovative OCLC load table rather than purchasing one from Innovative or creating one yourself. If 'OCM1' is not added, non-digit characters will be stripped and could overlay on a record with a matching OCLC number.

Perhaps some of these customization requests can also be handled by a local system. However, if you have a vendor to take some of your workload with no additional cost – why not? At this point CSUN has requested only two global changes: stripping non-LC subject headings, and setting first and second indicators of 776 (additional physical form entry) to 1 and blank. Both these requests were added as a result of the test record evaluation. Deleting non-LC subject headings was consistent with CSUN cataloging practice. Even if present these fields would not be displayed in public interface; but their absence would make the staff database much cleaner. Setting indicators in 776 to 1 and blank was caused by display and indexing issues in the Innovative system. CSUN also indexed $x (ISSN) of 776 to ensure ISSN detection by its SFX link resolver in case 022 in the record lacked another form's ISSN number.

Filling out the MARC profile concludes preliminary work for integrating SS records into the local catalog, and also generates a great sense of insatiable curiosity – how will those records look and how can we look at them?

To answer the first question, SS provides sets of sample records, configured according to the library's MARC profile, for the titles from the library's journal portal. Usually it is the first 500 records, but it can be a different number if requested. Because the sample comes from the first 500 records, alphabetically the records will end at the letter of the title of the 500th record. Once the file is prepared, SS e-mails it to the library.

How to review the records depends on the technological capacity of the library. The Getty Research Library has a test server that allows it to load records and examine them, including their public display, without ever risking loading the unknown into the production database. For libraries that have this facility, revision of the records is a simple and pressure-free task.

For libraries that do not have an additional server, CSUN among them, reviewing a large set of MARC records is a trickier but feasible task. In a situation like this libraries have two choices: load the records into the catalog and review them live or suppressed, or use MARC reader software, like MARCEdit, to look at the records without actually loading them.

Evaluation of test records: what to look for and what to expect

Compliance with the library's MARC profile

This is an obvious issue, and in CSUN's experience all its options and customization requests were fulfilled by SS from the first try.

General quality of MARC records and extraneous fields

As CSUN found out during the first load, most SS online records are based on the record for other forms of the publication, thus making the records a very distant cousin of what they would look like if CSUN cataloged the titles itself. However, all main access points were there (except in the brief records), and that was the most important issue. On the other hand, the records had many more MARC fields than CSUN would ever need or want. For example, there was a plethora of non-LC subject headings, which prompted CSUN to adjust its MARC profile after the first test load to strip all non-LC subject headings. The biggest concern was with title changes and whether SS would be able to handle them. Partly the worry was based on the fact that SS receives its data from the providers, and a title change in a library cataloging sense is a very different being from a title change in a vendor's interpretation. Vendors commonly use latest-entry practice and list all iterations of a journal under the most recent title, or change the title but continue to use the old ISSN. This results in SS using the record for earlier or later titles and adding a link covering both iterations. For example, in the record for *Proceedings of the Royal Society of London. Series A, Mathematical and Physical Sciences*, the publication dates state 1934–1990. However, the links have dates from 1905 to 1990, covering the earlier title *Proceedings of the Royal Society of London. Series A, Containing Papers of a Mathematical or Physical Character* (Figure 4.14). Figure 4.15 shows the MARC view of the record for this title. There was no record for the earlier title available in the SS knowledge base in this example. This somewhat justifies using one record to reflect dates coverage of earlier and later titles.

Figure 4.14   Example of SS record where coverage dates for earlier and later titles placed on record for later title

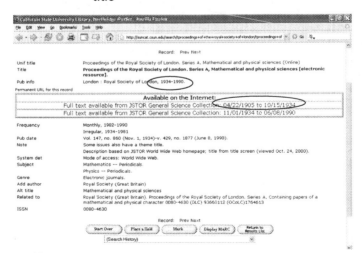

Source: CSUN online catalog

Figure 4.15 MARC view of record for title shown in Figure 4.14

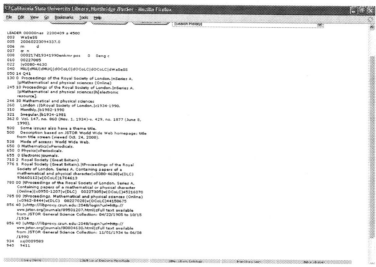

Source: CSUN online catalog

Another example of the downside of vendor-supplied bibliographic data about title changes is that the records may be split between different aggregations because different providers report them. One provider can have access to both versions but report only one title; another can provide access only to the later title and thus there is no need to list the earlier title. In this case, one of the titles may appear in an aggregation outside the library's subscription scope. An example is *Advertising Age's Creativity*, ISSN 1072–9119, which in 2001 changed title and ISSN to *Creativity (Crain Communications Inc.)*, ISSN 1541–3403. CSUN subscribes to both titles: the first is available from Lexis/Nexis and Factiva; the latter is available from databases outside CSUN's subscriptions. However, the record for the earlier title provides coverage dates that span both versions of the title, thus giving full coverage for the publication (Figure 4.16). Public display of the publication is shown in Figure 4.17. Even though the record for the later iteration was available from the SS knowledge base, it was not provided to CSUN as part of the load because LexisNexis in its communication with SS did not list the later title among its holdings.

Another disparity between publication dates and the URL coverage notes happens when a record for an online version that came later is used for access to the digitized version of the preceding print edition. Unless the library uses the single-record approach there is no apparent way to avoid unjustified hybrid information in the bulk-cataloging environment. The record for *Journal of Labor Economics (Online)* serves as an example of placing the dates of a digitized version of the print publication in the record for the online edition (Figure 4.18). The journal acquired an

Figure 4.16 Example of SS record where earlier title has coverage dates for later title

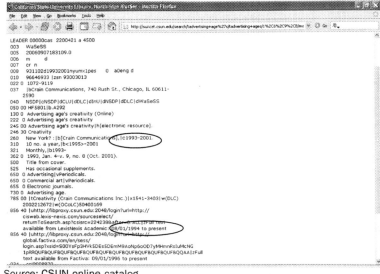

Source: CSUN online catalog

Figure 4.17 Public display of record shown in Figure 4.16

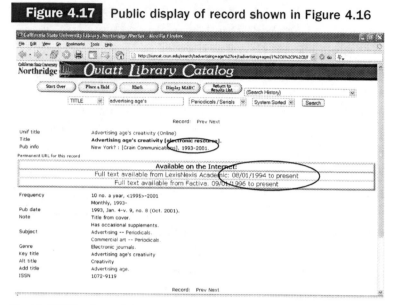

Source: CSUN online catalog

online counterpart in 2001; the links on the record point to the digitized version of the journal's print-only days, as well as the current electronic edition.

LexisNexis and Factiva

Most aggregations provide URLs that link from the record directly to the journal. Not so for the LexisNexis and Factiva databases. Their links take the user only as far as the general search screen of the database. In case of LexisNexis the interface's limits box gets prepopulated with the title of the journal, thus limiting the search to that particular title. As for the Factiva database, the link takes the user to the general search screen with no mention of the journal originating the connection from the library server.

Figure 4.18 *Journal of Labor Economics* record with mismatched publication and coverage dates for digitized print version and online version

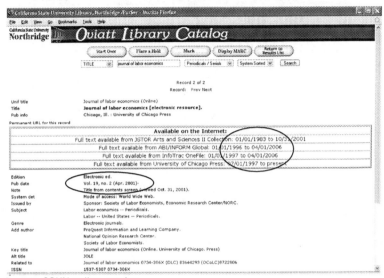

Source: CSUN online catalog

For this very reason, CSUN requested SS to order the links in such a way that the LexisNexis and Factiva links will be always at the bottom of the linking options in the record, making them the resources of 'last resort' for overlapping titles. Conveniently, SS was able to provide this customization (Figure 4.19).

Chronological order of coverage dates

The results of the evaluation showed that there was no particular sorting principle in the display of coverage information (with the later customized exception of LexisNexis and Factiva). Specifically, CSUN found it confusing not to have links in the chronological order of coverage dates, and requested customization of the display of links chronologically. Unfortunately, SS was unable to provide

Figure 4.19 Example of SS record with links displayed in customized order

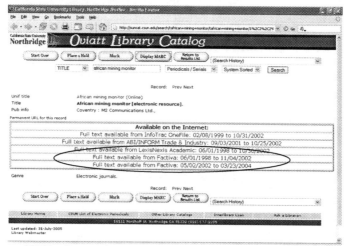

Source: CSUN online catalog

this level of customization. Recently, however, it was observed that CSUN's links got reordered chronologically. It must have happened over a period of time as records were changing. When SS was asked about this enhancement, it replied that no new algorithms were implemented and 'their system generates database order at random and therefore they cannot provide links in a logical order'.[6] It would be interesting to know if other libraries noticed a similar change or new libraries receive the records with links being in chronological order.

Linking

When supplying the test file, SS emphasized checking as many links as possible within and outside CSUN's IP ranges to ensure that proxy servers are working correctly. Most of the library's URLs were configured correctly and there was no problem linking as far as one could tell during the testing. Later on, however, CSUN came across a difficulty.

Thomson Gale databases

CSUN discovered a problem with these databases after loading the first trial records into its OPAC. One of the librarians tried to connect on campus to a Gale database (InfoTrac, Health Reference Center, etc.) and instead of seamless connection was prompted to the log-in. Having investigated the issue, the systems administrator determined that the SS URLs were wrong. Gale uses something called 'infomark' and these URLs were missing CSUN's site code.

This problem existed during the test load as well, but was not discovered because if a user connects to a Gale resource a cookie gets set on his/her computer enabling future seamless connections. During the record evaluation period the incorrect Gale URLs were compensated by the cookies that were present on the team's computers after earlier visits to Gale's website, thus masking the problem. Once a user tried to access the resources from a cookie-free computer, the user was prompted to the log-in. To correct the problem the infomarks needed to be appended with the library code. For example, an infomark for the title *3G Mobile* is:

> http://infotrac.galegroup.com/itw/infomark/1/1/1/
> purl=rc18%5fITOF%5F0%5F%5Fjn+%223G+
> Mobile%22.

The correct URL should be:

> http://infotrac.galegroup.com/itw/infomark/1/1/1/
> purl=rc18%5fITOF%5F0%5F%5Fjn+%223G+
> Mobile%22?sw_aep=csunorthridge.

Fortunately, SS is familiar with the problem of cookies and Gale URLs, and deals with it using what it calls 'URL straightners' – in other words appending library code to the infomark, which allows seamless connection to a Gale resource. In CSUN's instance SS re-ran a new file and supplied records containing correct links. To test the correctness of Gale URLs, the cookies need to be deleted from the computer. If using the Internet Explorer browser go to:

Tools→Internet Options→Delete Cookies.

Duplicate linking

The test load evaluation also revealed some issues with duplicate linking. One type of duplication was straightforward: some records contained two URLs for the same database and the same coverage dates. These were cleaned up by SS for the production load and did not reoccur in the library catalog.

The other type of duplication is trickier. It has to do with the subsets of the main aggregations, e.g. ABI/INFORM Global and ABI/INFORM Trade & Industry. In this case the links show different paths of access but in fact connect to the same web address. This type of duplication is caused by the fact that each subset of the larger package, including the package itself, is entered by SS under its own name and therefore a separate link for each is embedded into the record.

Figures 4.20 and 4.21 are an example of such duplication in the record for *Agency Sales (Online)*. Both links have identical URL syntax and therefore connect the user to the same website.

Figure 4.20 Example of SS record with two differing links connecting to the same website

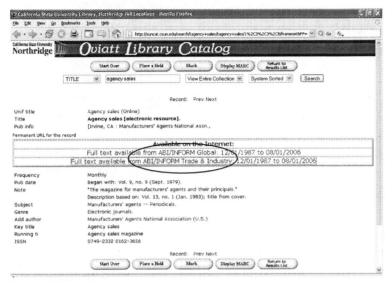

Source: CSUN online catalog

Figure 4.21 MARC view of record shown in Figure 4.20

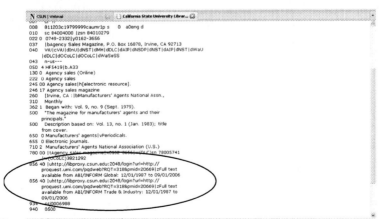

Source: CSUN online catalog

First production load

Once a library finishes its test record evaluation, it is ready to accept the first load. The first load is a complex one and requires several decisions.

How to load: overlay existing catalog records or duplicate them?

This question arises only if a library has previously cataloged some of its electronic journal titles. If so, and if the library used a single-record approach and then opted for separate records with SS, the obvious choice would be to load the records as an addition to the catalog and allow some temporary duplication. To suppress pre-existing records temporarily in order to avoid duplication of access is not a viable option in this case because it would also suppress print holdings.

The choice is less clear if the library retains its approach to e-journal cataloging with SS records. In the example of CSUN, it had previously cataloged about 5,000 e-journals using a separate-record approach, opting for separate records from SS as well. It was considering an overlay of existing records by incoming records from SS; for the overlay to occur there has to be a reliable match point(s) for the system to find any duplication.

The issue of the second and all subsequent load overlays was clear – all SS records have a unique title identifier embedded in the record enabling reliable overlay in the future. For the first load, however, CSUN tried to find a MARC field(s) that would provide 100 per cent match accuracy. Several parameters were considered, such as ISSN and title combination, GMD, etc., but CSUN ended up deciding against the overlay altogether. Some of the tags were not indexed by the system, and in the instance of ISSN and title the concern was that some journals do not have an ISSN and the title may be constructed differently in local and SS records. The team determined that the risk outweighed the benefit.

Strictly speaking the overlay could be a convenience but not a necessity in the initial load process. Once it was decided not to use the overlay, the next questions were whether to suppress either existing or incoming records or allow duplicate access to about 5,000 titles; and, if duplicate access was allowed, whether to undertake a clean-up project to eliminate the subsequent duplication.

Answering the second question first, the task force's unanimous decision was to undertake the clean-up project. The clean-up would entail finding the duplicate records, transferring local fields that the library wanted to protect/retain to the SS version and deleting the existing/suppressed record.

Suppression

Suppressing existing records seemed to be the easier task. This meant CSUN would have to run a file of the locally cataloged e-journals, which were expected to be duplicated by the SS load, and suppress them. Suppressing incoming records would entail loading them first and then searching and processing; thus suppressing 5,000 existing records was easier than suppressing about 20,000 records, the size of the initial load. In addition, suppressing existing records meant users would have access to 20,000 titles rather than 5,000 titles.

In the end CSUN decided against any kind of suppression because of a consideration that among the existing records there could be some that were not duplicates, and therefore suppressing them would eliminate them from the OPAC. Since duplication could be verified only during the manual clean-up, it was decided that it was better to have duplicate access to 5,000 titles than to lose access to some of the titles.

Nearing the first load, the list of issues to resolve also included creation of the item records, authority control and OCLC holdings.

Item records

Most systems, including Voyager and Millennium, have the automatic capability to create an item, or MFHD/item, record for bulk cataloging. CSUN's systems administrator configured the load in such a way that Millennium created and attached the item records with predetermined parameters to every SS record during the load.

Authority control

CSUN's authority control procedure includes running weekly new headings reports. Naturally, preparing to load about 20,000 new records it was concerned what impact this would have on its authorities' workload. The number of potential new headings was unknown and there was some trepidation that new headings resulting from SS would overwhelm the capacity of the headings reports. One option was excluding SS records from the authority workflow from the start. The decision was to try the waters by first loading only small number of records and running a test report.

Once CSUN received its initial record file containing about 20,000 items, only 100 records were loaded into the production system. This gave an additional opportunity to look at the records in the live system, check the links, discover the problem with Gale URLs described earlier, and run a new headings report. The load of 100 records generated 66 'first-time use' authority report headings, meaning about 13,200 new headings could be expected upon completion of loading the entire file. But since SS records are fluid and may leave the library database at any time, these records were excluded from the authority reports run by the system.

Once CSUN notified SS that it was ready to accept the first load of records, it took only a few days for the company to generate the file and send the notification. The first load consisted of the records contained in full-text and article aggregations; single journals and government documents were not included in the first stage of implementation. All single journals that CSUN subscribes to, about 1,800 in total, were previously cataloged in CSUN's system, so there was no pressing need to get records for them from SS and CSUN did not activate any of them in a 'single journals' database.

In the meantime, CSUN wanted to verify that it still had access to all the single journals and only then add them to its journal profile. Some issues typical for aggregations are valid for single journals as well – for example, a library can lose access and not be notified. But as opposed to aggregations that can be managed by PAMS, single journals are the responsibility of the library. They are added on an individual basis and deleted from the journal profile manually.

Government documents

CSUN is a selective depository for government documents published by the US and Californian state governments. It is mandated to provide free public access to government documents by state and federal law. SS has a government documents database (found under provider 'U.S. Government') containing about 300 journals. It is not the most current or accurate database because the US government does not supply information to SS; instead, the titles there come from customers who notify the company, and from SS itself.

Because CSUN did not know what to expect from the SS MARC record service on a continuing basis, it was hesitant to include govdocs for three reasons:

- collection development issues;

- inconsistent use of PURLs;

- CSUN's existing catalog records came from the GPO, which adheres to a single-record approach, therefore the anticipated post-load clean-up to eliminate duplication would be more complex than with regular publications.

As a subset of the broader issue of access to free resources and CSUN's responsibility as a depository library, the government documents database needed to be evaluated by the govdocs librarian. For overlapping/duplicate titles with the SS e-catalog the issue was the form of access; for new titles the consideration was whether adding them would change the scope of CSUN's govdocs holdings. The process of evaluation was, as acknowledged by the govdocs librarian, very useful as the SS database contained titles that were previously unknown to CSUN, and adding them broadened its holdings for agencies dealing with international issues.

GPO records have multiple PURLs (persistent URLs), connecting to the full text, TOC, etc. The PURLs guarantee provision of free and stable access; thus CSUN was concerned whether SS was to be able to maintain all PURLs in the record. As was discovered later, this concern was well founded. SS, as part of its workflow, always strips out any links present in the base record and adds the URLs from its client center. This means that if a government title in the SS e-catalog was available only from a vendor and not a part of the US government database, it would get a vendor URL.

This creates a two-pronged problem. First, the vendor URL may not provide free access to the government title; second, the coverage available through a government agency may be broader than from a commercial vendor. For example, *Morbidity and Mortality Weekly Report* is available from CINAHL (EBSCO) from 1998 to date, from Academic Search Elite from 1996 to date, but from the agency site via a PURL from 1982 to date (Figure 4.22).

Frequently GPO records contain more than one PURL, e.g. linking to TOC, full text and other parts of the publication. These will be stripped from the record leaving only one URL per title connecting to the full text.

Figure 4.22 Example of SS record for a government resource with varying coverage among commercial aggregations and government agency

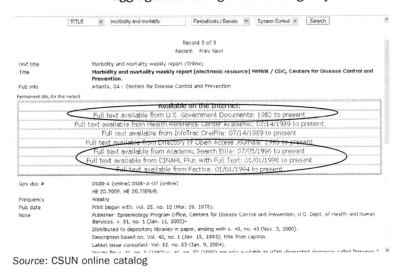

Source: CSUN online catalog

There is a partial solution to the PURL dilemma. If a government title comes in from a vendor database, the library can customize the URL as the PURL in the client center, which will trump the machine-assigned link. This of course may involve a lot of manual intervention, avoiding which is a major benefit of using PAMS. The SS portal allows only one URL per record to be customized. If there is a need to add more custom URLs, for example for TOC or to note the online location of the current issue, they can be added as a public note. SS can transfer the notes to any designated MARC field upon request.

GPO and a single-record approach

CSUN's biggest concern was a compound effect of the clean-up projects. Because of the difference in the approaches to its regular e-journal records and the govdocs, the clean-up project for govdocs had to have separate procedures and a different workflow. At the first stage of SS implementation it was decided to concentrate on the material that will be the bulk of the e-journal holdings, i.e. the titles in aggregations.

Looking back and knowing now that the records and linking work well, CSUN could have made the govdocs database part of its initial load and not have been overly concerned with losing free access or adding new titles outside of its scope. After all, the entire database size is only 323 titles!

Clean-up project

Without doubt cleaning up the duplication after the first record load was the least exciting part of the project. To begin the project CSUN created a file of e-journal records that existed in its catalog prior to the SS load and which it expected to be duplicated. The file, containing more than 5,000 records, was divided among five team members. To allow each person to work on their own file, five additional files were created, running against the master file. This way staff could monitor individual progress and be responsible for the assigned set of records. The implementation team developed the procedures, outlining steps in the process.

The SS duplicates clean-up project involves several steps.

- Search the title of locally cataloged journals and find the duplicate among SS records.
- Compare the URLs in old and new records and ascertain that all functional links are listed on the SS record. Note that the following providers should be considered the same (because of mergers/acquisitions):

Kluwer = Springer LINK

Ebscohost = Academic Search Elite

MetaPress = American Society for Clinical Pathology

Baywood Journals

Springer-Verlag (*not* Springer LINK)

Taylor and Francis Journals (the majority)

Transaction Publishers

- Transfer local fields that need to be protected in overlay from the old record to the SS record.
- Check if order record is present – if yes, transfer it to the SS record.

Not finding the matching title in the SS set could mean two things: a library's existing record is for a single non-aggregated journal, or a journal is not present in the SS database. The second scenario was more complicated. Since CSUN is part of the university system consortium, some of its packages are negotiated and paid for at the consortium level. Every year it gets the names of the databases and lists of the journals in them via spreadsheets from the chancellor's office. Every year a journal is listed according to the title it has that very year.

CSUN activates or uploads the spreadsheets to the portal with the titles the way they are listed in the consortium agreements for that year. However, many journals had a title change that was not reflected in the latest spreadsheet. At the same time there are many records coming from SS lacking but needing a 780 (preceding title) field to link to the earlier title. So if a journal is searched by its preceding title there may be no match found since the records are not linked. These 'orphaned' records require editing to indicate the 'continued by' relationship, i.e. adding 785, and one of the reasons to keep these records is that one still has perfectly good access to the earlier title.

De-duping e-journal titles was a very tedious and time-consuming task. Because of other competing work priorities it did not progress as quickly as hoped. In the end the project was transferred to a library school intern, who completed the task swiftly and effectively.

Maintenance

The biggest and most time-consuming efforts in the process of MARC records implementation are the work preceding the first load and the post-load clean-up. Routine monthly maintenance of the records, on the other hand, is an easy task that makes all initial efforts pay off.

SS sends a monthly e-mail (usually around the 10th of every month) notifying the library that an update is ready to be loaded. The update consists of three files: 'new', 'changes' and 'deletes'. At the library's request the company can combine 'new' and 'changes' into one file. The files come in the form of MARC records and their status is recorded in MARC LEADER_05. CSUN loads 'new' and 'changed' records automatically and the 'delete' records are handled manually.

One lesson to be learned about monthly updates is that if the library gets a subscription to a new journal package, its activation in the SS e-journal portal needs to be done quickly. Because the reality of a MARC records service was so new to CSUN, on a couple of occasions it missed activating a new database in time for it to be included in the monthly update, and so had to wait another month for the records to appear in its catalog. Since the update notification comes in only *approximately* at the same time of the month and one does not know exactly when the file is being run and how much lag time there is between the actual file creation and the e-mail, it is hard to gauge the cut-off date for a database to be activated. This, of course, would not be an issue for a library with a hosted links option, where update of the portal takes place daily.

Single journals

Single journals represent a picture of how the world of electronic journals looked before aggregators took over. The libraries know them by title, have control over every subscription and are more likely to be aware if a journal changes its title or ceases to exist; journals are also more likely to have been cataloged.

Everything that PAMS makes convenient for managing aggregations is inconvenient for handling single journals. They need to be activated/deleted one by one by the library in its journal portal if the title is part of the single journal database – otherwise they need to be cataloged manually. The other feature of these journals is that they have order records attached to them. This means that each goes through the cycle, starting with a bibliographer, going on to acquisitions and ending in cataloging. A wrinkle in processing single journals is how to incorporate them into the SS, or another PAMS, service.

CSUN has developed a workflow chart on how to do that. The main point is to activate the title in the SS knowledge base if it is present there. If the title is not in the SS e-catalog, the library has an option to suggest that it should be added to the database. In CSUN's experience, SS has been very responsive to these kinds of requests. If the vendor's record comes in as a 'change' record at some point, it will have no effect on the attached order because the bibliographic record will be overlaid without touching the order.

Frequently asked questions

While working on the MARC record service implementation the task force members learn all aspects of how the records work; they understand the issues behind display, linking and public notes. Librarians who are not part of the process, mainly public services, are one of the biggest beneficiaries of the service but do not and should not understand all the intricacies of implementation. They eagerly wait for the records to appear in OPAC and have preconceived notions on how the records should look. Their expectations are certainly formed by the level of manual cataloging done previously. Even if the library previously had vendor records in its catalog, most likely those were monographs and either came from the same source as records cataloged locally, i.e. PromptCat/OCLC, or look very similar to that. Vendor records for e-journals are of course a whole different story.

Once you load the records into the database, be prepared for an onslaught of questions from everyone who uses the catalog. It may be easier and less time-consuming to deal with them if the implementation team can be prepared in advance and draft a frequently asked questions (FAQ) document. Again, because of lack of experience CSUN did not anticipate the volume of questions that came, repeated by many colleagues. Shortly after the first record load the author found herself spending hours answering e-mails explaining why the records and links work a certain way.

Here are some questions and answers that may be helpful to libraries looking into implementing a MARC record service in starting their FAQ list.

- *Question*: Why do the coverage dates in the record show that our access starts in 1996 – when we connect to the journal our full-text access starts in 1998?

- *Answer*: Because SS assigns the coverage dates available for this journal in general by getting information from the provider, and does not customize dates for individual libraries. In this case, our subscription allows access only back to 1998, not 1996. We will do our best to customize date coverage with SS.

- *Question*: Why does our catalog record show that we have full text of a journal from a particular database, but when we go there no full text is available?

- *Answer*: Because the aggregator packages drop and acquire titles on a continuing basis, the aggregator must have dropped this title recently, but since we get updates only once a month this change has not yet been reflected in our catalog.

- *Question*: Why are there no subject headings in some records?

- *Answer*: Because some records are so-called 'brief' records; they are generated by the machine and have a very basic structure.

- *Question*: When linking from a citation using the SFX button, the SFX menu says that no online full text is available but the next line says that the library has this title – check the catalog. Clicking on the 'check the catalog' button the link takes you to the journal that is in fact available online! Why did SFX not show it as an online full-text option? We used not to have this problem – what is happening?

- *Answer*: The problem is occurring because the number of journals in the SFX knowledge base is substantially less (by about 10,000 titles) than the number of electronic journals in our catalog due to the larger size of the SS knowledge base. The lack of data synchronization causes SFX not to recognize that we have the title electronically; in this case SFX, after not finding the journal in its knowledge base, would do a default title search in the catalog and find the SS record, which in turn will link to the online full text. You come across this problem because our SS load created about a 10,000-title gap between the two databases.

- *Question*: Why do we have two records for so many titles?

- *Answer*: Because the SS load produced about 5,000 duplicate records from the combination of pre-existing records and SS records for the same titles.

These questions and answers are just suggestions, and may not reflect the issues specific to any particular library.

E-holdings

So you loaded the MARC records into your catalog and made them available to the library's users: the next logical question is will your library contribute these records to the consortium union catalog, if such exists, as well as the OCLC? In CSUN's case there is a union catalog, Pharos, for the California State University system. CSUN currently sends monthly lists of the library catalog's new and deleted records to Pharos, and plans in the future to contribute SS records as well.

As for the OCLC, for every e-journal CSUN preciously cataloged manually, it updated its holdings in WorldCat. Updating holdings for 20,000 records is not only an impossible task; it also prompts the question of keeping these holdings current.

After a two-year pilot project working with TDNet, EBSCO, SS and Ex Libris, and involving 21 libraries, in summer 2006 the OCLC unveiled a new service enabling automatic setting of e-journal title-level holdings in its WorldCat database. Libraries that use e-journal management services from any of the mentioned companies need to register for this monthly service with the OCLC and activate this option in their PAMS portal. The service uses ISSN as a match point and thus works only for journals that have ISSNs. The holdings' setting and updating takes place on title level and the library has an option of setting lend/not lend ILL policy. The service is free for PAMS customers and OCLC subscribers.

The benefits include a higher usability rate of the library's collection through OCLC First Search and Open WorldCat platforms. The library user gets access to online contents by searching an OCLC interface, not just the library's catalog. Since the holdings will also be visible in OCLC Resource

Sharing, ILL services may increase fulfillment through local institutions; on the other hand it will deflate ILL requests coming from the library's own patrons originating from WorldCat or First Search. When CSUN activated its e-holdings service, the ILL team was delighted because now they did not have to search for journals in OCLC and local catalogs – most of the time searching OCLC alone would satisfy their queries.

Many libraries took advantage of this service; others expressed some concern about lack of control over a library's holdings. When a library signs up for the service in the SS portal, the list of holdings to activate in the OCLC consists of the database titles. This means that every title in a database containing ISSNs to which the library has access will be checked off in the OCLC.

The newly introduced e-holdings service from PAMS and the OCLC represents the previously missing link in the workflow automated by the commercial electronic journal management companies, and one more convenience afforded to libraries through collaboration with commercial structures.

Notes

1 Collins, Maria H. (2005) 'The effects of e-journal management tools and services on serials cataloging', *Serials Review*, 31(4): 291–7.
2 Morris, Wayne and Thomas, Lynda (2002) 'Single or separate OPAC records for e-journals: the Glamorgan perspective', *Serials Librarian*, 41(3/4): 97–110.
3 Chen, Xiaotian, Colgan, Larry, Greene, Courtney, Lowe, Elizabeth and Winke, Conrad (2004) 'E-resource

cataloging practices: A survey of academic libraries and consortia', *Serials Librarian*, 47(1/2): 153–79.

4 Available at: *www.serialssolutions.com/promotion/ kb.pdf* (accessed: 10 September 2006).

5 Adoption of access-level record, or CONSER Standard Record, announced on pcclist@listserv.loc.gov, 20 November 2006.

6 Allison Feist, personal communication, 3 October 2006.

Current and future issues of cataloging

The role of the cataloger in the new millennium is drastically different from the old days. The explosive growth of electronic resources has brought an unprecedented challenge for catalogers. There has been a noticeable shift from 'deep' quality cataloging to 'light' cataloging. The process has evolved from creating or downloading single records, one at a time, to loading files of hundreds and thousands of records at a time. Cataloging has been 'super-sized'. While the idea of shared cataloging was revolutionary for its era, saving untold resources and duplication of work, the current climate demands bulk, batch and automated cataloging. And lack of cataloging – with all its drawbacks – does not necessarily mean that the resource is completely undiscoverable because access can be provided by other means, such as lists and link resolvers.

The technological developments in the information industry can compensate to a certain extent for a lack of cataloging. Very few libraries, stretched by budget cuts and overwhelmed by the sheer amount of material available, can afford title-by-title cataloging any longer. Quality seems to be yielding to quantity but, considering the progress in technology, perhaps the very notion of quality should be redefined.

Thanks to advances in electronic data harvesting and exchange, the sole source of catalog records is no longer limited to downloading them from the OCLC (and previously RLIN). Files of monographic records can be downloaded from book vendors, records for the ever-growing number of e-journals can be supplied by PAMS and many records can be automatically generated by machine. These records of course may not be of all-standard-compliant cataloging quality, but today's search engines can compensate adequately for the deficiencies of the supplied cataloging. In addition, more often than not the records coming from PromptCat, a cataloging branch of the OCLC, via a book vendor are the same records that would be downloaded manually in a title-by-title cataloging process.

Is the author joining doomsayers predicting the demise of cataloging as a profession? Not at all: simply pointing to a paradigm shift in the profession where a cataloger's knowledge of the principles of link resolution, indexing rules, loading tables and search algorithms outweighs the benefits of knowledge of AACR2 punctuation, correct abbreviations and the order of 500 notes. From title-level to bulk-level cataloging, from full-level record to access-level record, from library assistant to Web Cataloging Assistant, the changes are evident and irreversible. A host of new developments over the last few years make access to, and discovery of, the resources more powerful than ever before.

Metasearching

The term 'metasearch' has many synonyms: parallel search, federated search, broadcast search, cross-database search and search portal. All provide the ability for 'search and retrieval to span multiple databases, sources, platforms, protocols, and vendors at one time'.[1] Metasearch enables the information seeker to find data housed in numerous sources by using a single search interface (Figure 5.1).

A user may not be aware of the technical term, but will nevertheless yearn for the ideal of one-click searching across diverse resources, otherwise known as metasearching. Simplicity (or the least effort) of searching is an established preference of users. They do not care where the information comes from – they only want to find it. The phrase 'only librarians like searching, everyone else likes finding' became a cliché library joke. But as we know, there is a joke in every joke. Ideally metasearching could provide that simplicity to users and be a 'one-stop shop' to information resources. However, the success of federated searching is rooted in several conditions.

The provision of a single search interface to multiple sources can be attained via the Z39.50 protocol. In using Z39.50, 'one system translates a set of local commands into

Figure 5.1   CSUN metasearch webpage

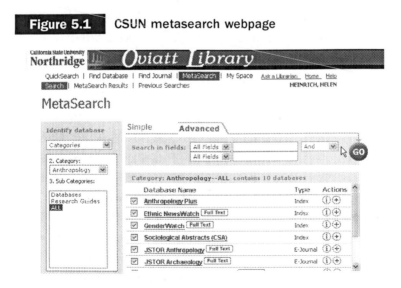

a set of universal commands that are then sent to another computer. The second system translates the universal commands into equivalent commands for the second system. The results are then returned to the first computer in the same fashion.'[2] In order to be 'metasearchable' the data have to be in a database that is Z39.50 compliant. For the metasearching to result in query resolution, the process follows several steps:[3]

- search

- retrieve

- merge/de-duplicate

- sort

- display.

With the potential of being a silver bullet for streamlining research, metasearching nevertheless has several limitations. In pointing out 'the bad' in metasearching while describing its implementation at CSUN, Helfer and Wakimoto state that 'not all databases are created equal or have the same standards. Some databases are not Z39.50 compliant... Even with Z39.50-compliant metasearching, you often cannot conduct the more sophisticated and complex searching allowed in some of the individual databases.'[4] When metasearching employs Z39.50, the protocol becomes the common denominator with standardized indexes. 'However, the mapping of specific fields to specific indexes does not take into account whatever special indexes may exist locally; nor does it consider any of the local indexing decisions.'[5] Having a Z39.50-compliant database and/or utilizing crosswalks for various metadata accomplishes only partial interoperability. It cannot make up for the differences in thesauri and the syntax of subject headings, therefore making the 'importance of vocabulary control and special indexes... obvious when searching across multiple databases in this manner'.[6]

Metasearching is a new and developing technology, and while not perfect it has a tremendous potential for libraries, because this is mostly what users want. Unfortunately what users 'want' is where libraries lose the battle to search engines such as Google Scholar, which is capable of retrieving results from numerous sources while providing a simple search interface.

OpenURL

The OpenURL standard is a syntax to create web-transportable packages of metadata and/or identifiers about an information object. Such packages are at the core of context-sensitive or open-link technology.[7] In other words, OpenURL is a linking protocol that carries metadata about an article from the citation to the full text. OpenURL not only links from a source (citation) to a target (specific article), but it does so through context-sensitive linking, i.e. it takes into account subscription restrictions, license agreements, coverage dates and other parameters.

Here is a demonstration of how OpenURL linking works in the example of an SFX link resolver. The user finds a record for the citation (Figure 5.2). By clicking on the FindText button the user is presented with the SFX server menu (Figure 5.3). Note how the metadata about the article from the citation find their way to the link-resolution menu.

Behind the scenes in this process is the knowledge base, where the library defines its collection, thresholds and other parameters. This is how the link resolver knows if the article is available to the library user. If the library has an ERM system which can be integrated with the link resolver, the

Figure 5.2   Illustration of OpenURL SFX linking, step 1

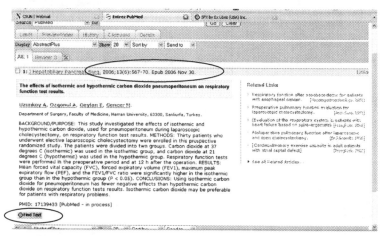

Source: PubMed free government database, accessed through CSUN library portal

Figure 5.3   Illustration of OpenURL SFX linking, step 2

Source: CSUN SFX menu

menu will display information about the particular journal (e.g. peer-reviewed) and the library's terms of use for this publication.

The link-resolver menu is under the control of the library as far as the choice of services it offers (e.g. citation formatting) and their wording. The library has an option of including electronic as well as print holdings in its resolver's database. In this case, it will point to the presence of a specific journal issue in its print collection. The institution also has a choice to bypass the menu altogether and offer direct linking from the citation to the full text.

Implementation of an OpenURL link resolver in a library will dramatically increase the usage of collections, making an excellent return on the hundreds of thousands of dollars invested in journal subscriptions. Some search engines, such as Google Scholar and Microsoft Academic Live, can be linked to a citation resolver, such as SFX from Ex Libris. Considering the number of students who do their research first and foremost on the internet, integrating a library's collection with the functionalities of these search behemoths will expose the library's resources to patrons who never thought about starting their research from the university library's homepage. We may say that we are better than the internet, but are we more popular? And as they say, if you cannot beat them, join them.

OpenURL linking is a young technology and is not always perfect. Some of the challenges include non-OpenURL-compliant databases, such as Factiva, where the user will be presented with the search screen instead of the article. But even with OpenURL-compliant databases the linking sometimes hits a snag. The process is based on matching the information from the source to the target, and if the data are incomplete or incorrect at either end the linking fails.

The OpenURL framework introduces new opportunities and challenges: standardization of data elements; expanded scope of linking opportunities; a larger set of services becoming possible; and a potential for new applications such as linking to simulations of scientific experiments. Until now OpenURL has been seen as an end-user system, but there are possibilities for its use as server-to-server communication.[8]

CrossRef

Another type of citation-to-full-text linking can be executed by using a digital object identifier, or DOI.

> A DOI is an alphanumeric name that identifies digital content, such as a book or journal article. The DOI is paired with the object's electronic address, or URL, in an updateable central directory, and is published in place of the URL in order to avoid broken links while allowing the content to move as needed.[9]

DOI-based linking is administered by CrossRef, a non-profit membership organization established in 2000 in cooperation with leading scholarly publishers and the International DOI Foundation.[10] When an article is published, the publisher submits metadata about it to CrossRef along with its DOI and corresponding URL. CrossRef maintains a database of matching DOIs and URLs. If the publisher moves contents to another platform or undertakes other changes resulting in a non-functioning URL, the publisher simply updates the DOI directory; the DOI itself never changes, which means that all the links to that content which have already been propagated still function.[11]

DOI-based linking cannot determine if the library has access to the article. However, there is a synergetic relationship between DOI and OpenURL linking. CrossRef is OpenURL compatible and DOI can be part of OpenURL. In this case, the OpenURL link resolver will determine article availability. On the other hand, if linking occurs directly through DOI and the DOI server is OpenURL aware, it will recognize if the user has the right to access the article contents.

Open access

The open access (OA) movement came about as the result of the library and academic community fighting back on the price hikes of scholarly journals imposed by publishing conglomerates. Profit margins grew by 20–40 per cent per year, pacing the levels of luxury market goods such as fine jewelry, yachts and expensive cars.[12] The rising prices outpaced the rate of inflation, cost-of-living increases and growth of library budgets. By 2000 libraries could no longer maintain the constant level of serials subscriptions and began a steady cutback in coverage, in addition to paying more for the journals to which they continued to subscribe.[13]

The shift of control in the dissemination of scholarly knowledge from scientists, scholars and libraries to publishers marked a crisis in scholarly communication. But in the mid-1990s an international movement within the scholarly community emerged to win back control over academic communication and capitalize on the opportunities presented by the internet for new electronic publishing.

Steve Harnad's 1994 paper[14] is considered the seminal event for the OA initiative. Harnad suggested that scholars publish their preprints of unpublished, unrefereed, original work on a globally accessible archive, freely available to scholars with network access anywhere in the world. When a work is formally published, authors will substitute the published work for the preprint. Hanard made the point that scholars need not withdraw preprints from public viewing after refereed versions are accepted for paper publication. Once this process becomes common, journal publishers will be forced to restructure their costs for electronic-only versions to be truer to actual costs, which he estimated to be 25 per cent less than paper page costs.[15]

There are several recognized statements on open access. The most commonly used are the Budapest Open Access Initiative[16] and the Bethesda Statement on Open Access Publishing.[17] The International Federation for Library Associations defines OA publications as follows:

> An open access publication is one that meets the following two conditions:
> 1. The author(s) and copyright holder(s) grant(s) to all users a free, irrevocable, world-wide, perpetual (for the lifetime of the applicable copyright) right of access to, and a license to copy, use, distribute, perform and display the work publicly and to make and distribute derivative works in any digital medium for any reasonable purpose, subject to proper attribution of authorship, as well as the right to make small numbers of printed copies for their personal use.
> 2. A complete version of the work and all supplemental materials, including a copy of the permission as stated above, in a suitable standard electronic format is deposited immediately upon initial publication in at least one online repository that is supported by an academic institution, scholarly society, government agency, or other well-established organization that seeks to enable open access, unrestricted distribution, interoperability, and long-term archiving.[18]

There are two issues in the OA initiative: one has to do with archiving OA scholarly information; the other concerns publication of scholarly research through OA journals.

Open Archives Initiative

There are numerous ways for authors to archive their works. The works can be stored in institutional repositories, authors' personal websites and disciplinary archives. The compatibility of the data is in the purview of the Open Archives Initiative (OAI),[19] which develops and promotes interoperability standards that aim to facilitate the efficient dissemination of content. The OAI has its roots in an effort to enhance access to e-print archives as a means of increasing the availability of scholarly communication.[20]

In order for the archived scholarly information to be searched in a systematic manner, the OAI developed the Open Archives Initiative Protocol for Metadata Harvesting (OAI-PMH), releasing the first version in 2001. The participants in this interoperability project provide and harvest data in the OAI-PMH format so the researcher can seek information by using a single service provider. The OAI maintains a list of data providers (those who expose data for harvesting in OAI-PMH format) and service providers (those who harvest metadata from data providers and make them available on their sites).[21] Currently there are 529 data providers and 23 service providers.

Among OAI service providers are the Sheet Music Consortium[22] from the University of California, Los Angeles, Scirus,[23] a search engine concentrating on scientific content, and CYCLADES[24] from the European Research Consortium for Informatics and Mathematics (ERCIM). But the best known and one of the first is OAIster,[25] a project from the University of Michigan Libraries (Figure 5.4).

Open-access journals

Open-access journals perform peer reviews and then make the approved contents freely available to the world. Their expenses consist of peer review, manuscript preparation and server space. OA journals pay their bills very much the way broadcast television and radio stations do: those with an interest in disseminating the content pay the production

Figure 5.4   OAlster homepage

costs upfront so that access can be free of charge for everyone with the right equipment. Sometimes this means journals have a subsidy from the hosting university or professional society; sometimes journals charge a processing fee on accepted articles, to be paid by the author or the author's sponsor (employer, funding agency).[26]

OA journals can be listed in the *Directory of Open Access Journals (DOAJ)*.[27] The directory is operated by Lund University Libraries (Sweden) and currently lists 2,450 journals. OA journals are also included in A&I services and serials management services, such as Serials Solutions, provide MARC records for them.

There are several major organizations that publish and archive OA journals:

- Biomed Central (www.biomedcentral.com) currently lists 168 peer-reviewed OA journals;

- FreeMedicalJournals.com lists 1,460 journals;

- SciELO (www.scielo.org/index.php), the Scientific Electronic Library Online, lists 279 journals in Spanish and Portuguese;

- Public Library of Science (PLoS);

- SPARC (www.arl.org/sparc/), the Scholarly Publishing and Academic Resources Coalition, lists and aggregates the sources of OA journals.[28]

When the OA initiative was introduced there were some concerns about the longevity of OA journals, the sustainability of the free-access model and the effect of OA journals on scholarship. However, a study of 86 OA journals published in 1995 found that 57 per cent were still published in 2001,[29] a rate comparable to that of print journals. According to findings by Oxford University Press,[30] examining the usage of OA journals using the example of *Nucleic Acids Research (NAR)*, a molecular biology journal owned and published by OUP, the 'use of *NAR* has changed – and dramatically', noting an increase in usage of 143 per cent from January 2003 (when the journal went OA) to January 2005. One conclusion made by the report is that the 'growth in article usage was powered by the use of free articles'. The use of non-OA fee-paid articles remained relatively static during this period. For all three years the top four issues were free. The study also concluded that OA contributed to an additional increase in usage of about 7–8 per cent with a significant increase in newer article usage. OA also brought in new users, 'especially people from the Eastern Bloc and possibly also students'. As far as the visibility issue is concerned, many people may not even know that OA exists for current OA materials, and as people become more aware there could be a further surge in use.[31]

As awareness about OA journals grows, so does their popularity. In 2006 the *DOAJ* reported that visitors from more than 150 countries use the service monthly and hundreds of libraries worldwide have included its titles in their catalogues.[32]

The future of cataloging

Is this an oxymoron? Does cataloging have a future? One could wonder, reading the action items identified at the 2006 joint BIBCO/CONSER Operations Meeting and listed under Strategic Directions of the Program for Cooperative Cataloging (PCC):[33] 'The group recommended changing "Program for Cooperative Cataloging" to something else that excludes "Cataloging" and includes "Metadata" or "Shared Metadata," or "Sharing Metadata," or "Metadata Sharing".'[34] It can be argued, though, that sharing metadata is in fact cataloging in cooperative fashion. Michael Gorman pointed out the false dichotomy between metadata and cataloging back in 1999.[35] Considering that participants at the meeting are the foremost authorities in the field, knowing the essence of the issue, the author would interpret the suggestion for the name change as a change in semantics bowing to the demands of the technical vocabulary of the twenty-first century, or rather contemporizing the name and pushing the profession into the relevancy of the new millennium. Once a reference librarian, obviously surprised by the author's enthusiasm about the cataloging profession, asked why cataloging was not considered 'sexy' in library school, The author has never thought about cataloging as 'sexy' (as opposed to sexiness of public services?) but has also never thought it was considered 'unsexy'.

The name change of the PCC, the stalwart of cataloging, will definitely have an effect on the names of courses in library school. As it is, cataloging departments around the country get converted into metadata centers. If the change goes through it will have an even broader impact on cataloging terminology around the country. 'Advance Course in Metadata Creation' – Reference, beat that! So goodbye PCC, hello Program for Metadata Sharing?

Looking five to ten years into the future of cataloging, Carlen Ruschoff, director of technical services at the University of Maryland Libraries, PCC strategic plan adviser and author of the visionary statement *Cataloging, Discovery and PCC's Future* as part of the PCC strategic planning process, predicts that:

> human intervention in the preparation of metadata for use will be greatly changed and vastly diminished within libraries. Batchloading of metadata from publishers will foster the creation of mechanisms for data integrity and 'piece tracking' for both the tangible and the electronic acquisitions. The skill sets of catalogers will evolve from a rule based set to a deeper understanding of how metadata may be exploited by search engines and providing valuable information in the development of discovery tools. Cataloging records for materials will be created only when electronic metadata packages are not available... Catalogers' duties will shift to assisting with the development of metadata of quality assurance tools and workflows, being a part of the development of metadata harvesting tools, and, of course creating metadata when there is none available. In addition, catalogers' skills are likely to be employed in digitization programs and the creation of metadata that goes along with such programs.[36]

Beacher Wiggins, LC director for acquisitions and bibliographic access, foresees that:

the number of authors, creators, publishers, and vendors who will supply cataloging/metadata along with their intellectual and commercial output will grow. Complementing these suppliers of metadata will be the automated tools that will assist in the harvesting, extraction, or generation of needed cataloging/metadata.[37]

Web Cataloging Assistant

An example of such an automated tool is the Web Cataloging Assistant[38] (or WebCat Assistant) from the LC's Bibliographic Enrichment Advisory Team. The project has been concentrating on providing online access to social science monographic series available in electronic form. The team members determined which series were available online and added the URL link to the serial record. The next step in the process, the creation of the individual monographic record, was significantly automated. Catalogers examine the abstract page for a particular monograph on the web and, by using the Web Cataloging Assistant computer and programmed functions, automatically create and add a MARC record to the LC catalog. This record includes an abstract of the title represented. The records are subsequently enhanced by a cataloger to ensure the presence of name headings and subject headings. Automating the manual processes speeds up the creation of the record and enables a cataloger to concentrate on the intellectual work.

AMeGA project

WebCat Assistant is a practical step illustrating the broader direction for the LC towards automation of bibliographic control of web resources. According to Section 4.2 of the LC

Bibliographic Control Action Plan, there is a need to 'develop specifications for a tool that will enable libraries to extract [and harvest] metadata from Web-based resources in order to create catalog records and that will detect and report changes in resource content and bibliographic data in order to maintain those records'.[39] To that effect the LC sponsored the creation of the Automatic Metadata Generation Applications (AMeGA) project,[40] whose final report became available in February 2005.[41] The project was charged with identifying recommended functionalities for automatic metadata generation applications. Its recommendations cover the following categories:

- system goals;
- general system recommendations;
- system configuration;
- metadata identification/gathering;
- support for human metadata generation;
- metadata enhancement/refinement and publishing;
- metadata evaluation;
- metadata generation for non-textual resources.

While the full automation of metadata generation belongs to the domain of the future, there are strides under way that will expedite 'human metadata generation'. The development of access-level records has advanced from monographs and integrating remote records to include serial records as well.

Access-level records

Access-level records represent an adjustment of cataloging to the reality of remote resources, as well as an increase in the cost of cataloging and number of materials to be cataloged. The concept of an 'access-level' record came from an internal LC workgroup in 2004: the idea stemmed from the reality that the descriptive elements of the full record might not be useful, and often redundant for a description of the remote resources. Functionally, an access-level record is meant to emphasize the elements that aid in access to the resource, as implied by the name, and de-emphasize the traditional elements that do not support resource discovery.

The purpose of an access-level record is to support user tasks: to find, identify, select and obtain, as defined by FRBR. Having been reduced to the essential, this level of elements also achieves a decrease in cost and increase in productivity of cataloging without compromising the resource discovery process. In addition there is a substantial diminution of the training period required for catalogers working with access-level records. The guidelines defining the creation of the record comply with current cataloging rules. The following elements are *not* to be included in the access-level record:

- 041
- 043
- 245 $b, $c
- 246 $i
- 247 $f
- 250 $b
- 260
- 300
- 310
- 362
- 490
- 500 (source of title)

- 500 (source of edition)

- 500 (item described)

- 500 (justification of AE)

- 504

- 505

- 530

- 76x–78x, other than preceding/succeeding

- many 008 positions.[42]

Figure 5.5 shows an example of an access-level record.

After evaluating the results of a test of access-level records conducted between December 2004 and January 2005, the LC decided to continue applying the new model to non-serial remote-access electronic resources, distribute records via regular distribution channels (Cataloging Distribution Service), solicit feedback from the libraries and consider whether the 'access-level' model might also apply to other types of resources.[43]

Figure 5.5   Example of non-serial access record

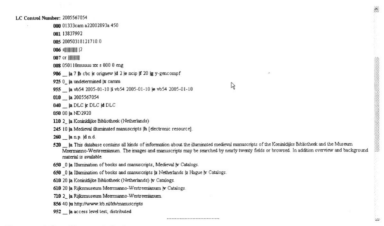

Source: LC online catalog

The formation of the Access Level Record for Serials Working Group charged with the development of a single CONSER access-level record was an outgrowth of the access-level record for monographs and integrating remote-access electronic resources. The record objectives of the serial access-level record match those of remote integrating resources in terms of functionality, cost-effectiveness and conformity to the current cataloging standards. The new level of serials cataloging would apply to all formats and replace existing multiple-record levels, and reduce serials cataloging costs by requiring in the records only those elements that are necessary to meet FRBR user tasks.[44] The working group developed and tested the mandatory-element set via a pilot project conducted in 14 libraries; results showed that time saved varied by institution, ranging from lows of 5 per cent and 14 per cent (Stanford, Harvard) to highs of 30–35 per cent (UCLA, Georgia, GPO, LC). The average time saved in the creation of serial bibliographic descriptions was 25 per cent.[45] Following feedback from the libraries participating in the test project, the group adjusted the element set and cataloging guidelines. The target date for implementation was November 2006. The mandatory elements are summarized below:[46]

- selected leader and fixed field codes;
- control or identification numbers (ISSN, LCCN, CODEN) and 042 code;
- main entry;
- abbreviated title;
- titles: title proper, variant titles, former titles;
- edition statement;
- publisher;

- place (originally in limited cases, later made mandatory);
- extent (field 300), required except for print and online resources;
- current frequency;
- date/designation (all unformatted);
- specified notes: source of title, DBO, LIC, reproduction, system details (limited), language notes, index notes;
- subject and name added entries;
- most linking fields;
- series added entries (only if SAR is made);
- series statements (required only if no SAR is made);
- URLs (as specified).

The omitted elements were as follows:[47]

- 008 22 except for microforms;
- 008 18–19 (frequency, regularity);
- distinguishing uniform titles (except for generic titles, monographic series);
- other title information, statements of responsibility (generally);
- parallel titles from 245 (retained in 246);
- place of publication generally (later reinstated);
- added entries that duplicate linking fields;
- series statements (if SAR and added entry are made);
- series added entries (if no SAR is made);
- extent (field 300), not required for print and online resources;
- formatted beginning and ending volumes and dates (362); all will be unformatted;

- many notes, including 321, 580, 550, 440;
- 006 and 007: all but first two bytes;
- 730, 740, 787.

Figures 5.6 and 5.7 show a comparison of the elements set between control records and access-level records.

There is a noteworthy conclusion at end of the final report of the working group. It outlines the rearrangement of priorities in cataloging, shifting the emphasis away from scrupulous description, which in the near future may be fully automated, to the 'findability' or discovery of the resources in principle. The value of our catalogs will be determined not by the quality of record descriptions but by the quantity of the resources contained in the catalog. The more materials we can provide through our catalogs, the more relevant they will stay to our users.

> There can be little doubt that we are living in times of change, both within and outside the library universe. It is hoped that the development and implementation of

Figure 5.6 Example of serial control record

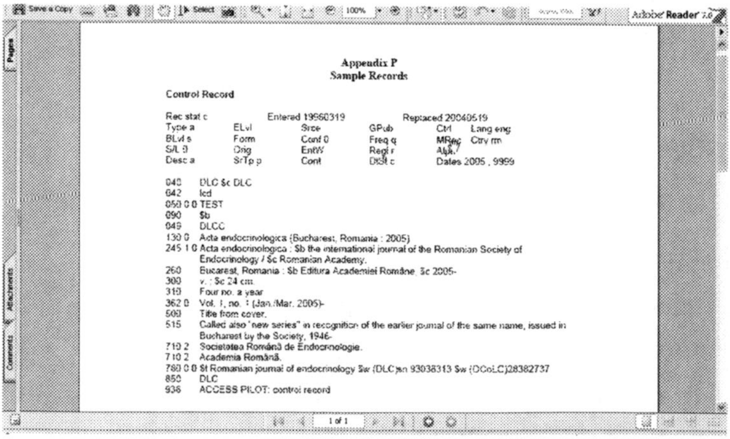

Appendix P
Sample Records

Control Record

Rec stat c		Entered 19960319		Replaced 20040519	
Type a	ELvl	Srce	GPub	Ctrl	Lang eng
BLvl s	Form	Conf 0	Freq q	MRec	Ctry rm
S/L 0	Orig	EntW	Regl r	Alph	
Desc a	SrTp p	Cont	DISt c	Dates 2005 , 9999	

040 DLC $c DLC
042 lcd
050 0 0 TEST
090 $b
049 DLCC
130 0 Acta endocrinologica (Bucharest, Romania : 2005)
245 1 0 Acta endocrinologica : $b the international journal of the Romanian Society of Endocrinology / $c Romanian Academy.
260 Bucarest, Romania : $b Editura Academiei Române, $c 2005-
300 v. : $c 24 cm.
310 Four no. a year
362 0 Vol. 1, no. 1 (Jan./Mar. 2005)-
500 Title from cover.
515 Called also "new series" in recognition of the earlier journal of the same name, issued in Bucharest by the Society, 1946-
710 2 Societatea Română de Endocrinologie.
710 2 Academia Română.
780 0 0 $t Romanian journal of endocrinology $w (DLC)sn 93038313 $w (OCoLC)28382737
850 DLC
936 ACCESS PILOT: control record

Figure 5.7 Example of serial access-level record

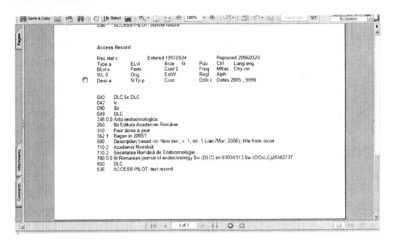

this new standard record for serials will lead serials cataloging down the path of learning and change required to remain cost effective while providing significant value (e.g. controlled name access and controlled vocabulary subject access) that cannot as yet be provided in any other way. The Working Group recognizes that the changes required by this new record may challenge the flexibility of some of our colleagues and may seem to some to devalue the meticulous work and documentation that past practices required. However, many of the ideas embodied in this record were proposed by practicing catalogers, and almost half the Working Group consisted of catalogers. Many of the catalogers' proposals were supported by the analysis that the Working Group performed to evaluate elements according to FRBR user tasks.

While there can be some justifiable sadness at leaving behind what might one day be regarded as a 'golden age of cataloging', such a move seems almost overdue in light of the current economic and digital environment. The Working Group therefore urges the speedy implementation of the recommendations in this document as a crucial step towards avoiding the possibility that catalogers might otherwise 'find themselves beautifully equipped for a world that no longer exists'.[48]

Conclusion

In the good old times library collections were measured by their quality and size. The march of information technology and emergence of electronic resources changed that paradigm. For an average user the ways in which a library provides access to its collections becomes equally, if not more, important than the collections themselves. Library technology provides the power to maximize the use of library resources. The value of a great collection may be diminished if the user cannot access its electronic resources remotely, if articles 'buried' in the databases may never be found but for the link resolver connecting citation to source. A search may never be pursued elsewhere in the collections if the item was not found in the catalog. If the collection is not woven into the web through Google Scholar, MS Academic Live or Open WorldCat, a library may never know how many of its own users it has lost.

On the other hand, the robust implementation of technology, facilitating access to the resources, can considerably make up for the size of the collection. It can enable patrons to search every virtual nook and cranny of the library and increase the likelihood of satisfying a user's needs.

The underpinning of the seamless-access technology is the presence of data in various information silos of the library. Libraries are a vast marketplace for technology and data vendors; vendors, in their turn, are vital for library services. As electronic technology progresses, this symbiotic relationship is becoming tighter and tighter. The proliferation of electronic data exchange has an osmotic effect on the library/vendor partnership.

Libraries used to be the undisputed champions of information organization and provision of metadata in general. The advent of the internet and the explosion of information resources exposed two weaknesses in the library dominance of the metadata market. The first is the inability to manage, on our own, the sheer volume of information that needs to be encoded and organized. The invasion of the catalogers' world by electronic journals and aggregator packages very quickly left us feeling helpless in trying to win the upper hand in establishing bibliographic control over online resources. The vendors, however, could afford to concentrate just on that and provide libraries with electronic journal management systems and MARC records sets, maximizing libraries' investment in electronic serials collections.

The second weakness of metadata creation that undermined a library's monopoly was the lack of metadata standards for use in the marketplace. In addition to inventorying books and transporting bibliographic data, vendors needed to sell and to make money. And the MARC format was not conducive for the commercial spread of books. Thus the publishers and vendors themselves developed standards for description, such as ONIX, which now can be used for data exchange between publishers, third parties and libraries.

ONIX for Serials is being developed jointly by the publishing and library communities with the clear goal of providing non-library metadata for library use. In the not-so-distant future ONIX for License Expressions, the metadata for legal license agreements under development by EDItEUR, will also be populating library ERM systems, along with ONIX subscription information.

The development of SUSHI (Standardized Usage Statistics Harvesting Initiative)[49] further illustrates the tightening cooperation between libraries and commercial information services. A committee representing libraries and information vendors is working together on ways to provide consolidated machine-to-machine harvesting of COUNTER-compliant statistics on the usage of electronic resources.

In addition to cooperation, repurposing and adapting vendors' data for library use, online content providers will exert a further influence on the way we provide bibliographic control. Driven by the bottom line and not the cataloging rules, commercial enterprises will adapt their publishing business models to the opportunities presented by the networked environment.

How long will journal aggregations remain 'journal'. There is really no necessity from the user's viewpoint to maintain the structure of the online serial entity. It is only a matter of time before the aggregations will represent the growing collection of articles identified only by title and author. How will catalogers maintain bibliographic control of these publications? What rules will be applied? Will we be ready? Will we be ready when electronic books become collections of chapters? Or maybe 'chapter' aggregations will be on an equal footing with article aggregations?

Libraries, especially catalogers, should anticipate and be ready for the changes in a world where transformations take place at the speed of a computer transaction.

The trend for further collaboration with commercial content and data providers, the adoption of mutual standards which strengthen the communication lines and the exchange of ideas need to be extended to broader areas, even the inner sanctum of the profession – the development of new cataloging rules. Otherwise, if we develop new rules in the absence of commercial publishing and content provision, not accounting for changing business models in the real world, we may find ourselves with squeaky new rules and very few areas in which to apply them. And then what do we do? As Gloria Steinem once asked, 'If the shoe doesn't fit, must we change the foot?'

Notes

1 Available at: *www.niso.org/committees/MS_initiative .html* (accessed: 18 February 2007).
2 Taylor, Arlene G. (2004) *The Organization of Information*, 2nd edn. Westport, CT: Libraries Unlimited.
3 Baca, Murtha (2004) 'Integrated access and metasearching: introductory remarks', paper presented at MCN 2004, Minneapolis, 12 November; available at: *www.mcn.edu/conference/MCN2004/delegate/presentations/ BacaMCN2004MetasearchIntroduction.pdf* (accessed: 18 February 2007).
4 Helfer, Doris and Wakimoto, J.C. (2005) 'Metasearching: the good, the bad and the ugly of making it work in your library', *Searcher*, 13(2): 40–1.
5 Woodley, Mary S. (2000) 'Crosswalks, the path to universal access?', paper presented at Introduction to Metadata, Getty Research Institute, Los Angeles, August; available at: *www.getty.edu/research/conducting_ research/standards/intrometadata/path.html* (accessed: 18 February 2007).
6 Ibid.
7 Available at: *www.niso.org/committees/committee_ax. html* (accessed: 18 February 2007).

8 Apps, Ann (2004) 'The OpenURL and OpenURL framework: demystifying link resolution', *Ariadne*, 38; available at: *www.ariadne.ac.uk/issue38/apps-rpt/* (accessed: 18 February 2007).

9 Available at: *www.crossref.org/03libraries/16openurl .html* (accessed: 18 February 2007).

10 Morgan, Cliff (2004) 'Metadata for STM journal publishers: a review of the current scene', *Learned Publishing*, 17: 31–7.

11 Available at: *www.crossref.org/03libraries/16openurl .html* (accessed: 18 February 2007).

12 Yiotis, Kristin (2005) 'The open access initiative: a new paradigm for scholarly communications', *Information Technology and Libraries*, 24(4): 157–62.

13 Ibid.

14 Harnad, Steven (1994) 'Scholarly journals at the crossroads: a subversive proposal for electronic publishing', *ARL Issues in Scholarly Communication*, June; available at: *www.arl.org/scomm/subversive/ sub01.html* (accessed: 5 November 2006).

15 Yiotis, note 12 above.

16 Available at: *www.earlham.edu/~peters/fos/boaifaq.htm* (accessed: 5 November 2006).

17 Available at: *www.earlham.edu/~peters/fos/bethesda .htm* (accessed: 5 November 2006).

18 Available at: *www.ifla.org/V/cdoc/open-access04.html* (accessed: 18 February 2007).

19 Available at: *www.openarchives.org* (accessed: 18 February 2007).

20 Available at: *www.openarchives.org/organization/index .html* (accessed: 18 February 2007).

21 Available at: *www.openarchives.org/community/index .html* (accessed: 18 February 2007).

22 Available at: *http://digital.library.ucla.edu/sheetmusic/* (accessed: 5 November 2006).

23 Available at: *www.scirus.com/srsapp/* (accessed: 5 November 2006).

24 Available at: *www.ercim.org/cyclades/* (accessed: 5 November 2006).

25 Available at: *http://oaister.umdl.umich.edu/o/oaister/* (accessed: 5 November 2006).

26 Suber, Peter (2004) 'A brief introduction of open access', 29 December; available at: *www.earlham.edu/~peters/fos/brief.htm* (accessed: 5 November 2006).

27 Available at: *www.doaj.org/* (accessed: 18 February 2007).

28 Available at: *www.arl.org/sparc/partner/index.html#list* (accessed: 18 February 2007).

29 Crawford, Walt (2002) 'Free electronic refereed journals: getting past the arc of enthusiasm', *Learned Publishing*, 15(2): 117–23.

30 Peek, Robin (2006) 'The Oxford University Press on OA', *Information Today*, 23(8): 17–18.

31 Ibid.

32 *Information Outlook* (2006) 'DOAJ titles – pass 2,000', *Information Outlook*, 10(5): 9.

33 Available at: *www.loc.gov/catdir/pcc/-* (accessed: 8 November 2006).

34 Available at: *www.loc.gov/catdir/pcc/draftstratdir.html* (accessed: 8 November 2006).

35 Gorman, Michael (1999) 'Metadata or cataloging? A false choice', *Journal of Internet Cataloging*, 2(1): 5–22.

36 Ruschoff, Carlen (2006) *Cataloging, Discovery and PCC's Future*; available at: *www.loc.gov/catdir/pcc/2010html-* (accessed: 8 November 2006).

37 Wiggins, Beacher (2005) *Program for Cooperative Cataloging: A Vision and Direction*, 20 October; available at: *www.loc.gov/catdir/pcc/poco/VisionStatementWiggins.html* (accessed: 8 November 2006).

38 Available at: *www.loc.gov/catdir/beat/webcat.html* (accessed: 18 February 2007).
39 Available at: *www.loc.gov/catdir/bibcontrol/actionplan .pdf* (accessed: 18 February 2007).
40 Available at: *http://ils.unc.edu/mrc/amega* (accessed: 18 February 2007).
41 Available at: *www.loc.gov/catdir/bibcontrol/lc_amega_ final_report.pdf* (accessed: 18 February 2007).
42 ALCTS Electronic Resources Interest Group (2005) 'It's all about access!', paper presented at ALA Annual Meeting in Chicago; available at: *www.loc.gov/ catdir/access/ala_erig.ppt* (accessed: 18 February 2007).
43 Available at: *www.loc.gov/catdir/access/accessrecord .html* (accessed: 18 February 2007).
44 Available at: *www.loc.gov/acq/conser/alrFinalReport .html#charge* (accessed: 18 February 2007).
45 Available at: *www.loc.gov/acq/conser/alrFinalReport .html#mand* (accessed: 18 February 2007).
46 Ibid.
47 Ibid.
48 Available at: *www.loc.gov/acq/conser/alrFinalReport .html#concl* (accessed: 18 February 2007).
49 Available at: *www.niso.org/committees/SUSHI/SUSHI_ comm.html* (accessed: 18 February 2007).

Index

Printed in the United Kingdom
by Lightning Source UK Ltd.
121179UK00002B/115-120